# DREAMS

RUGARE GOMO

# DREAMS

## FORGING MY OWN PATH

*Advantage* | Books

Published by Advantage Books, Charleston, South Carolina.
An imprint of Advantage Media.

ADVANTAGE is a registered trademark, and the Advantage colophon is a trademark of Advantage Media Group, Inc.

Printed in the United States of America.

10  9  8  7  6  5  4  3  2  1

ISBN: 978-1-64225-915-5 (Paperback)
ISBN: 978-1-64225-914-8 (eBook)

Library of Congress Control Number: 2024910291

Cover design by Megan Elger.
Layout design by Matthew Morse.

This publication is designed to provide accurate and authoritative information in regard to the subject matter covered. It is sold with the understanding that the publisher is not engaged in rendering legal, accounting, or other professional services. If legal advice or other expert assistance is required, the services of a competent professional person should be sought.

Advantage Books is an imprint of Advantage Media Group. Advantage Media helps busy entrepreneurs, CEOs, and leaders write and publish a book to grow their business and become the authority in their field. Advantage authors comprise an exclusive community of industry professionals, idea-makers, and thought leaders. For more information go to **advantagemedia.com**.

*For all of those who dare to Dream.*

# CONTENTS

# CHAPTER 1

# Dreaming: The Grass Is Greener on the Other Side

## A Stubborn Boy in a Hopeful World

From the moment I entered the world, the world told me I did not belong. My name is Rugare Gomo, which means "God's Peace." However, my story is far from godly. I was born at 5:20 p.m. on Sunday, September 23, 1984, at Norwich Hospital in the United Kingdom. My parents were expecting a baby girl, and I was to be named Ruva-Rashe Gomo, which means "God's Flower." To their surprise, I was a boy.

I was born stateless to Zimbabwean parents, and I was neither a British nor a Zimbabwean citizen. My parents were students in the United Kingdom, and in 1983, the British had changed the immigration laws, which ceased the automatic acquisition of British citizenship at birth unless the parents were already British citizens or had the right of indefinite stay. Since I was not born in Zimbabwe, the Zimbabwean government did not grant me automatic citizenship either.

Right from the start, I did not fit the arbitrary laws of this world. These laws never consider the devastating consequences to babies being rendered stateless, and still today, millions of children around the world like me are rendered stateless: the children born into refugee camps in Kenya, children born to noncitizens in Estonia or Latvia. Over time, I've learned that not all people are born equal, and for many, it is the place of birth and the passport in hand that determine the opportunities and quality of life one has. The moment I was born, the world was determined to rob me of my future.

I only spent one year and eight months in the United Kingdom before my parents returned to Zimbabwe after my dad had completed his theological training. We were dirt poor, living in a tiny home in a shantytown called Tshabalala in Bulawayo—Zimbabwe's second largest city. While I have few memories of my time living there, a few have marked my mind and stayed with me over the years.

I must have been around three, and my grandmother, Mbuya Mutukumira (my mum's mum), was staying with us. I was playing a game of putting a stone in my nose and blowing it out hard. Mbuya Mutukumira told me to stop, but I wouldn't until a stone got stuck up my nose. I remember thinking that this stone would be stuck in my nose forever. It felt like hours before Dad got back from work, and he figured a way to get the stone out of my nose. This was likely one of the first times my family realized how stubborn I could be.

Another memory was when my parents were at work, I would go into their bedroom, find my mum's bright red nail polish, and paint my toenails. I knew to remove the nail polish before they got home so I would not be caught, but I insisted on wearing it so I covered it up by putting on socks, but they always seemed to be privy to my red toenails.

I believe I was stubborn because I never doubted who I was deep down inside. Beneath all the layers I have piled up over the years, there was always that core part of me, the part that beat in the center of my heart. When I was three years old, I was effortlessly cutting my meat and feeding myself because I did not want anyone else to have to help me.

It was as if my life started when I was four years old. I don't remember much before that age. What stands out most about this memory is that I was such a young child, but I remember so vividly how I knew who I was. The idea that I was in control of my future and the confidence I had in making decisions for myself is something that was so clear to me because I was raised in a culture where children should be seen and not heard. At four years old, my father took me on a motorcycle ride, and I remember loving every second of that ride, from the way the long T-shirt flapped in the wind around me like a dress, to the way I clung to my father, to the way it felt to be trusted to go for such a ride. I can still feel the sun penetrating my face as I clung to my father while he drove us through the busy streets of Tshabalala, turning the tight corners with the ease of a professional, as we flew down the narrow streets lined with shacks and houses.

Not long after I turned five, we moved to Mutare, the fourth biggest city in Zimbabwe at that time, with a population of around three hundred thousand. Dad had been made the regional director of Scripture Union and the move came with a beautiful home. It was an old light-blue colonial with high roofs, wooden floors, two verandahs, and a backyard.

We had a new start in life. Everything needed updating, and my family and I set to work in transforming this property into our home. We built a chicken coup and several vegetable gardens, and we looked after so many different animals—dogs, chickens, rabbits, pigeons, guinea pigs, cats. It was a happy home with a small animal farm in the inner city.

## Navigating the World through the Lens of Fear, Disconnection, and Loneliness

Belonging is something that is innate in all of us. We want to be part of the pack, so when it came time for my older brother to go to school, naturally I wanted to join him. I cried and begged my parents, starting a morning ritual that involved me pleading to go to school in a sing-song voice. At the time, I was just under five, and I really didn't know what I was asking for, but I knew that my brother was going to school, and I wanted to join him. Finally, as the year passed, I was eligible to start going to school. It only took me half a day of school to realize that I hated it, and from the second I got in the building, I sensed something was wrong. I told myself the reason it felt wrong was because I didn't belong.

The kids were speaking Shona, the most common language in Zimbabwe, but not the language I had grown up learning. Unlike most kids of my age, my first language was English. My parents made a conscious decision to raise us to speak English as our first language because they believed it would give us opportunities in life. Because I had been surrounded by English-speaking friends and family members and we went to an English-speaking church, I assumed the majority of people would be English speakers. I was wrong. So, when I went to school, I was not armed with the language that would allow me to connect to my fellow classmates and I had trouble keeping up with what was going on in the classroom. Outside of school, I had heard people speaking Shona, but my family spoke mostly in English, so I never had to learn to speak Shona, yet every one of my classmates was speaking that language.

On the first day of school, the teachers asked if anyone was born in a different country. There were four of us born outside of Zimbabwe. This was surprising for me. Our friends at church came from diverse backgrounds so my experience had told me that some people were born in Zimbabwe and others were born in different parts of the world. I had assumed many people in Zimbabwe were from outside Zimbabwe. Being singled out this way at school made me feel different. Since I could not connect with the other kids, I do remember telling myself that I must be special. This decision I made at five years old would be the context of a life of fear, disconnection, and profound loneliness.

## The Mothers Before Me—Building a Legacy on Their Foundation

I come from a family of strong, progressive women who didn't fear breaking the traditional rules and culture in a male-dominated society. My mother's father, my grandfather, was a polygamist. He had three wives, and the third wife was my grandmother. People in the village thought my grandmother was bewitched because she had a disability. Many years later, they realized that she had polio as a child, which had left her leg deformed. The villagers believed she was lucky to be married at all, considering "she was bewitched." In Zimbabwe, like in many countries, women had no rights and they belonged to the husband and the children belonged to the father. The entire order of society is based on the man, their view, and their needs, and there are zero exceptions. My grandmother had two children, first, my mum, Rosemary Mutukumira, and then my uncle, Chris Mutukumira. When the Christian missionaries came to Zimbabwe, they wanted my grandmother to be educated. At the time, she was ten years old. My grandmother's father did not value women, so he told the missionaries to educate my great uncle, Sekuru Todd, instead. Sekuru Todd got the education that my grandmother was denied.

Mbuya Mutukumira defied society's expectations of what a woman was allowed to do in the village. Her mission was to ensure my mum obtained an education that she herself was denied. Mbuya left her husband and returned to her village with my mum and uncle so they could go to school. This was unheard of in rural Zimbabwe in the fifties. She raised my mum and uncle like a single mum. My grandmother was entrepreneurial, and she spent much of her time sewing clothes and traveling the country selling them. She toiled the land and became a master farmer, winning awards for growing quality cotton and maize. All these things she did so that my mum would have a better future than she had. My grandmother chose the hardest of roads for the possibility of a new life for my mum.

Mbuya Mutukumira was known in the village for going against the grain. She had impatience for dumb men. The women in the village would tell me that if she had an education and had been a man, she could have been the chief of the village. She was smart, bold, spoke her mind, and stepped outside the cultural norms to live in the changing times. My legacy is built upon her foundation.

My grandmother's hard work paid off when my mum became one of the six girls to attend secondary school. There weren't many career opportunities for women during my mum's days. Unlike my uncle who could be anything he wished because he was a man, my mum had two options: to be a nurse or a teacher. After completing secondary school, my mum trained as a nurse. Irrespective of the limited opportunities my mum had because she is a woman, having an education gave her a life most of her peers never got to have. In Zimbabwe, due to severe poverty, some parents resort to giving their young daughters away (aged fifteen to eighteen) for marriage in return for money or cattle. In Zimbabwe, about one in twenty women were married before the age of fifteen, and one in three before the age of eighteen. My grandmother ensured that my mum would have a choice regarding her future, and her education reduced the pressure of being given away for marriage like her cousins, allowing her to have a choice in who she wanted to spend her life with. My mum eventually chose to marry my dad.

An educated woman is more likely to recognize the importance of education and ensure her children get one too. Before my mum chose to marry my dad, she made him promise that all the children would have the opportunity for education. My brother was the first of us to go to university, where he obtained a degree in computer science. He now lives in America and is constantly headhunted for his expertise in cybersecurity. My sister is the first female in my family to have completed university in finance and accounting at the University of Cape Town in South Africa and is currently working through the CFA (Chartered Financial Analyst) exams, which are some of the toughest exams in the world. I was the first in my lineage to attend high school and complete university overseas. I have a double degree in arts and law from Monash University in Australia. I am a lawyer, now an author, high-performance life and business coach, and a businessman. All of this is possible because my grandmother defied society's expectations and dared to work extremely hard to provide an education for my mum. My siblings and I are the first in our lineage to break many glass ceilings, our lives built on the foundations of my grandmother and the pillars of my mother.

Living in Australia, I hear so many people say things like, "I will quit my job when I have more money," or, "I can't pursue my dreams now because I have children," or, "I can start looking at how to be happy when I have paid my mortgage." My grandmother did not have the luxury for her circumstances to change, to bring her vision to light. What I have learned from her is that I am responsible for changing my destiny, which takes commitment, hard work, and defying society and cultural norms. I learned that the world isn't going to change for me; I must change in order to change the world.

## A Foreigner in My Own Country

My journey to Australia did not happen in a vacuum. The values I acquired in our family home, books, television, and interacting with foreigners led me on an adventure of a lifetime.

It all starts in our home. And for me, it started with my mum, who is avant-garde. My mum trained as a nurse and her education has helped thousands of people. In the early nineties, Zimbabwe had the highest number of HIV infections in the entire world, and one in four adults were diagnosed as HIV positive. My mum was one of the first women doing HIV/AIDS education in the nineties in a male-dominated world. In those days and still in some parts of the world today, being HIV positive was a death sentence and it carried a lot of stigma. Those who were positive

**My journey to Australia did not happen in a vacuum. The values I acquired in our family home, books, television, and interacting with foreigners led me on an adventure of a lifetime.**

were ostracized from society. From the time I was eight years old, my mum used her life reaching out to the most vulnerable communities, including sex workers, truck drivers, and over 100,000 men working in mines. She walked into communities where she was not wanted and used her education and voice to save Zimbabweans and other Africans. My mother never once allowed her life to be limited by her gender.

My dad worked for Scripture Union, a nondenominational Christian organization that ran youth leadership programs, family counseling programs, and street kid programs. My dad was passionate about youth leadership programs, and like my mother, he modeled the importance of making a difference in the community, teaching me the impact of consistent commitment and dedication.

Reflecting on my childhood, our home was not a typical Zimbabwean home. It was a loving home where everyone was welcomed, and my parents modeled inclusivity and diversity before these terms became "woke." Because they treated everyone with love and kindness, they were viewed as community leaders. I remember when they welcomed a girl into our home right after she discovered she was HIV positive. Our open doors would attract street kids and fighting couples who would seek marriage counseling from my parents. Their unconditional love spread through the community like wildfire and encouraged others, particularly me, to do the same.

In Zimbabwe, girls are relegated to doing the house chores like cooking, looking after the children, washing clothing and dishes by hand, ironing, sweeping the house, and polishing the floors. Boys on the other hand had the sole priority of studying and getting good grades. My parents raised us different than the norm, and my brother and I were taught to do everything. There was no such thing as a girl or boy chore in our home. My mum taught me to sew, mend clothes, knit, and cook. My dad taught me to cut the grass, raise the chickens, and do the gardening. This was very unusual for our uncles and aunts who came to visit, who would freely lecture my parents on how wrong they were in how they raised us. Gender, in our home, was essentially irrelevant and boys and girls did everything.

When you grow up in a country like Zimbabwe, education is life-sustaining. A lack of education is poverty. As social workers, my parents were not rich—yet they did everything they could to expose us to the world. My parents fostered a culture of reading in the home. I could read and write by the time I was five. I remember fondly my mum teaching me to read the *Key Words with Peter and Jane* books. As we grew up, my brother and I were voracious readers. We read Enid Blyton books like *The Famous Five* to *The Secret Seven* and adventure stories like *The Hardy Boys* and *Nancy Drew*. We devoured all the books we could in our home, and when we ran out of books, we went to the library. We had one library in my city, and on the weekends, we would go as a family and would always undoubtedly be one of the few Black people there. For me, the library was heaven—a portal to worlds I thought I would never be able to go to. Zimbabwe, being a former British colony, had many old books from the nineteenth and early twentieth centuries. I devoured the books like *Biggles*, *The Wiggles*, *Gimlet*, and British stories of finding new lands and fighting wars. At school, we read Charles Dickens, Shakespeare, and Sherlock Holmes. My books taught me that there was a bigger world than my home city Mutare and that there wasn't just one way to live life.

Television also played a critical part of my upbringing. There wasn't a thing known as today's "binge watching." Instead, we tuned in to very specific programs, my dad often encouraging us to watch the BBC and CNN world news. This was how we consumed global affairs and adapted to global thinking. These were the days when we could mostly rely on the accuracy of world affairs, the days when the world shared the same information unlike today where who knows what is really going on. Even cartoons from overseas proved to be teachers in my childhood. I was entranced by *Captain Planet and the Planeteers* because it had the vision of the world I wanted to see: people from all walks of life coming together to make the world a better place. It was one of the few cartoons in my life that even had an African character. I was represented for the first time. I loved the Care Bears. They taught me kindness. The X-Men taught me to be inclusive of difference and not to fear difference. I could go on and on and on. Unfortunately, today, TV is not the same. In my days, TV was created to teach us values, to elevate the consciousness of humanity, and to question how we treat others. Today, TV seems to be about ego, drama, and the lowest parts of ourselves. Growing up, TV called on us to move in the direction of greatness.

Meeting people from different cultures and countries had a huge impact on how I think. The nearest thing to interacting with different cultures outside of Zimbabwe was through church, where many British people attended. My mother and father were viewed by the community as social workers, which brought many other cultures into my home, as many of the programs were foreign funded by organizations like Tearfund, USAID (United States Agency for International Development), churches, and volunteers around the world. We had the fortune of volunteers from the United Kingdom, Canada, Australia, and United States, and mostly English-speaking countries come to volunteer in my mum or dad's work and stay in our home. I loved it. Meeting people from other countries was my opportunity to learn about their life, their dreams, and their world. The conclusion as a child was that power was in the West because it was the West coming to help us in Zimbabwe. I wanted that kind of power. The power to make a meaningful difference in the world.

The way I was raised, the books I read, the television I watched, and my interactions with other cultures made me feel like a foreigner in my own country. I felt out of place. I thought differently. I wanted to find my people, my tribe, and I was certain they were somewhere out in the West. I idealized the West as a place of freedom, ideas, social responsibility, equality, and opportunity. I had made my decision.

## Saving Lives through Women's Higher Education

Allow me to mansplain why higher education for women saves lives. Mbuya Mutukumira, my grandmother, had a third child that died after two weeks. They thought he had been bewitched and nobody talked about it. Mum, being one of the very few women in the village to go to nursing school, learned that there were many babies dying in Zimbabwe with the same symptoms as my uncle: shallow breath and the shakes. My mum got to know this illness as tetanus, which, unlike in those times, is preventable by vaccine today.

In my grandmother's village, when babies were born, there was a ritual to pour mud onto the umbilical cord. My mother learned that it was this ritual that led to my uncle's death. You see, tetanus is a bacterium that lives in the soil and in animal waste that enters the body through a cut or open wound. My grandmother learned from my mother that her baby boy hadn't been bewitched at all. Instead, he had died from tetanus due to the ritual.

It is wild to think that one generation ago, my family members were dying from diseases that are preventable because of vaccinations. I am always grateful for the miracle of vaccines, the miracle of science that gives hope and saves lives. The lack of vaccines and access to medical care have had devastating effects on the people of Zimbabwe. In the 1990s, I grew up in the province called Manicaland with a population of about 1.5 million. At that time, the biggest city of Manicaland was Mutare with a population of about 300,000. There was only one public hospital for the entire province. During those days, there was only one pediatrician, who we all knew as Dr. Foster. Now, in Australia today, with a population of about twenty-five million, there are about 700 public hospitals and 650 private hospitals with a total of 3,000 pediatricians.

In the past, there were no mobile phones or landlines, and there was no access to information, doctors, or medicine, which meant that access to child healthcare was practically nonexistent. As a result, many children died as new diseases ravaged the community. Still today, in Zimbabwe, most people are subsistence farmers and live in the village with no running water or electricity. In fact, people have access to more mobile phones than clean drinking water.

Growing up in Zimbabwe, we understand the importance of vaccines and the investment in medical research. Vaccines save lives. During the COVID-19 pandemic, it was painful to watch groups of people in "developed countries" protesting vaccines and it high-lighted the regression of education in Western countries. The rigor and standards of education have plummeted. We no longer require our society to be versed in history, science, and literature. I am not saying the context of medical research and the role of pharmaceuticals is moral. We have *huge* problems there. But, taking the case of vaccines in isolation, they work, and they work imperfectly.

My mum's higher education allowed her to help other women understand key health issues that directly affect them. In a society that treats women as commodities, my mum is respected and consulted on key decisions, providing a valuable viewpoint on community matters, including those specific to women. My grandmother dared to break the cultural norms while providing the resources for my mum to be educated. My mum, without seeking power and glory, has a more empowered life because of her education.

Education makes the world a better place and allows all human beings to be actively engaged in change and progress. Perhaps the cure for cancer is in the mind of the girl in rural Zimbabwe, but that cure will not see the light of day because someone deemed girls are less valuable than men.

## Launching into a New Life

From as far back as I can remember, I fantasized about leaving Zimbabwe and finding my tribe. I spent a lot of my life daydreaming of going overseas and always imagined I would end up in the United Kingdom, the country of my birth. After all, my mother's tongue is British English, our national exams in Zimbabwe were British (the Cambridge National Exams), the books we read were British, and the TV we watched was British. I grew up with the British Anglo-Saxon worldview. Getting an opportunity to go to Great Britain for me was the highest form of living.

My parents would never be able to afford an education overseas. I knew that if I wanted to leave Zimbabwe, I would have to create my own opportunity, and I spent a lot of my time as a child trying to create it. Because this was pre-Internet times and my family didn't get a phone until I was thirteen, opportunities were created by approaching people and writing letters. In my mind, the best solution for creating opportunities was by simply asking people I knew. The problem, though, was that I didn't know anyone in the United Kingdom with whom I felt an emotional connection with. There was no one to ask, which was disheartening. I couldn't figure out how to open the door to the new life I dreamed of and that is when it occurred to me that I would need to change my thinking.

I was so attached to going to the United Kingdom that it made me blind to what I *really* wanted to achieve. What I did know was that I wanted to leave Zimbabwe and go to the West, so I let go of my attachment to going to the United Kingdom and grew open to different possibilities. There was one country where I had a connection, and that was Australia where Uncle Andrew lived.

## One Person Can Change Your Destiny

When I was five, the man I grew to call Uncle Andrew came to volunteer where my dad worked at Scripture Union. He is not a blood relative of mine; however, we became close while he stayed with my family for three months, and in Zimbabwean culture, those who are close to the family are typically called Uncle or Aunty. Uncle Andrew loved his time so much in Zimbabwe and other African countries that he continued to return to Zimbabwe, becoming a staple in our family home.

Uncle Andrew took me to my first day of school, he taught me and my brother how to make hamburgers and pull pranks, including a splattering cake for my mum's birthday, which we still laugh about today. Uncle Andrew also took my family on holidays we would never be able to afford otherwise, including The Victoria Falls, one of the seven wonders of the world, and a safari to Hwange National Park. I always thought of him as the big white man roaming the world and bearing gifts. He was free and fun, and he treated people kindly, just like the characters in the books I read.

I made the decision to ask Uncle Andrew if I could come stay with him in Australia next time he came to Zimbabwe. At just fourteen years old, I knew what I wanted and set a plan in motion. Knowing that Uncle Andrew visited once a year, sometimes only every other year, I was well aware that it could take me a long time to get an answer, so I needed to start immediately. I started by pestering my parents every time they got off a call with him. "When is Uncle Andrew coming back to visit?"

The answer was always, "I don't know," to which I was always disappointed. I couldn't tell my mum and dad why I was so curious about his arrival because I believed they wouldn't understand and would just consider me a dreaming child. And that I was. I had dreamed of going to high school in Australia, and I had limited time to get the ball rolling.

When we finally had a date for his arrival, I had it all planned out. My blend of emotions swirled within, causing an uproar of nerves. If he said yes, I would be ecstatic, bolstered by possibility. But if he said no, I would sink into hopelessness.

I have been asked many times what a "no" would have meant for me when I was fourteen years old. No meant I would never be free. I would have to live in Zimbabwe, in a country I mostly did not share the same value system, how they treat women, how children should be seen and not heard, how there is only one narrow path to live life.

- No meant living in fear each day that maybe someone was going to beat me up because I sounded and acted differently.
- No meant that I would be without a tribe. If I stayed in Zimbabwe, I would be isolated and lonely.
- No meant I would have to conform to the standards and ideals, the expectations and the morality of my family, my community, and my country.

- No meant I would be ostracized, deprived of opportunity, beaten up, and side-lined. To be an outcast meant no future, no hope. There is no point of living if hopelessness was my guaranteed future.

When the van pulled up in front of the house, I was filled with anticipation. Now, my heart sank and I felt like my whole life was crushing into me. Unknown to me, there had been a last-minute decision that Andrew's business partner Jennine, whom I have known since I was eight years old, would come instead of him.

Looking back, it's interesting to think about how this one diversion of my plan sent me on a downward spiral. I immediately thought my dreams were lost, like a popped bubble in the air, and I was going to have to follow the trodden path and my life was going to be a living hell. As I wallowed in self-pity and became consumed by negative thinking, it dawned on me that I could write a letter to Uncle Andrew and give it to Jennine. This was my last hope.

I pulled a chair from my desk. Brought it to my wardrobe and pulled down the typewriter. I had taught myself to touch type and this occasion required a typed letter. I typed a note. I crumbled it up because I wasn't happy with it, threw it away, started typing another one, and crumbled it up again. I don't know how many more I went through, all the while wasting expensive paper. I gave myself a pep talk and pushed myself ahead, knowing that it was now or never.

I approached Jennine and asked her if she could deliver the letter to Andrew. She obliged with excitement and brought it back to Australia when she departed, but I was once again filled with fear that it would not get into his hands, nervous that others would find out about my "secret" plan.

I waited for Uncle Andrew's response. An entire month went by without one. During this period, I was still going to school, and I remember being very distracted. I was completing my first two years of high school, known as the Zimbabwe Junior Certificate (ZJC). Afterward, I had to take a national exam to determine what my options were for my O-Level subjects (the next two years of high school). Another exam to be boxed into someone I am not. Nobody knew what I was dealing with. Absolutely nobody—no friend, no acquaintance, no family member. Nobody knew. The only person who knew that a letter had been written was Jennine. But she did not know that all my hopes, dreams, and aspirations were contained in this letter.

Every day I would check the letterbox to see if there was a response from Andrew. There was nothing. During that time, there had been discussions about me going to boarding school for my third year of high school. When the headmaster finally agreed, I said I didn't want to go. My dad couldn't understand why I changed my mind, but I thought to myself, "If I go to boarding school, that means I won't be at home to either receive a letter or work on my plan to go to Australia." So, I created space for this opportunity, but didn't know whether it was actually going to happen or not. I had my whole life riding on this letter. I was already making future decisions about my life based on something I had no idea was going to happen.

Two and a half months went by and the tension inside me had escalated. Three months went by, still nothing. Then, one day my dad came home and said to me, "What's this about you going to Australia?" My heart started racing. I didn't know how to respond. I didn't know if he was angry at me or whether he was excited. He wasn't showing much emotion, but I smiled at him cheekily and said, "I wrote a letter to Uncle Andrew to ask if I could go to Australia." My dad looked at me with happiness in his eyes saying that Uncle Andrew had said, "Yes, why not?" I was so filled with joy.

# Uncle Andrew's Response to My Letter (May 13, 2000)

*Dear Rugare,*

*I read your letter with excitement and astonishment, which you so well typed, and brought back by Jennine. Now ... you're continuing education. I have been pondering this one—and YES—I can't wait for you to come. There are several excellent schools within close proximity of my home, and I would love to be your "Uncle" while you study hard here. Clear boundaries would need to be discussed/set, as life here is sooooo different to Zimbabwe, and one could get very distracted!*

*What now ... you have a lot of battles, appointments etc etc with the Australian High Commission in Harare. Naturally, I will phone, fax, email them pledging your support here—to say that all will be looked after. But people from "developing" nations—it is hard to get visas to come here.*

*Would you be thinking of coming for one year, two years ... what is your bigger picture? I would need to set times to review everything, like finances, you fitting in here etc etc ... I know, and remember you as a fantastic person, and would hate the assumed wealth, freedom, etc to corrupt you!*

*Do not take NO as an acceptable answer from the Australian High Commission. You have no time to waste—it will probably take every waking day between now and January 2001 (school starts on the 26th of January) to get you here ... Are you ready for a fight?*

How did I feel about Uncle Andrew's email? To have someone say that they will stand by me and use their time, their money, their connections, and their energy to give me a new life was overwhelming, exciting, and scary. This "yes" to my dream was the beginning of a new path and the stakes were high. Failure was not an option. Uncle Andrew was willing to fight for me, so I had to fight for myself and for the possible life I saw ahead of me.

## Preparing for Battle

Uncle Andrew was right. There was no shortage of obstacles blocking me from Australia. From my family to my school, my nationality, money, age, and even the beliefs I held about myself, there were so many hurdles I'd have to jump to get the life I longed to lead.

My mum was in Nigeria when the news about me potentially going to Australia arrived. She was training Nigerians on an HIV/AIDS prevention program. Dad and I went to pick her up from the airport in Harare. On the three-hour car ride home, I remember Dad broaching the subject about me going to Australia. At first, Mum seemed lukewarm about the idea. She had concerns about a Black boy being in a predominantly white society—a society where the white Australians habitually discriminated against its First Nations people. After all, both my parents had experienced being the only Black family in Ipswich in the UK in the eighties. Right away, I assumed my mom's reaction meant that I would not be allowed to go, but she overcame her own concerns by looking at reality: They knew Uncle Andrew well and had met many of his friends who would be part of my community, including Aunty Jennine, Aunty Sharon, Nancy, and Dr. Price. They knew there would be great opportunities for me in Australia and agreed that I should go.

*I learned that people would have their reactions to the things I do in life, but it is my job not to buy into people's fears or concerns. My job is to pursue my dreams even if they disappoint the people I love the most.*

Uncle Andrew was faced with most of the obstacles, and his first one was finding a high school for me that he could afford. Because I was an international student, my tuition would be pricey.

In Australia, going to a government school is free for most students or the school fees are nominal. Uncle Andrew wanted me to go to a Christian school. The first he looked into was Oxley College, which would cost $15–$20K a year. This was prohibitive. We were both very disappointed. For my family, that could be a decade of savings. Uncle Andrew approached the government schools, and they advised that the school fees would be $8,000 per year. While more reasonable, this was still very expensive for Uncle Andrew. His last stop was a school near his home, called Kingswood, which cost $16,000 per year. The headmaster at the time said that they had never had an African in the school before and, to increase the school's diversity, offered me a part scholarship, dropping my fees to $6,000 per year. What I learned as Uncle Andrew accepted the offer was to never give up on the first "no."

**I learned that people would have their reactions to the things I do in life, but it is my job not to buy into people's fears or concerns. My job is to pursue my dreams even if they disappoint the people I love the most.**

As you may remember, despite being born in the United Kingdom, I was declared a noncitizen by the British government, and I was declared a noncitizen by the Zimbabwean government. Being stateless meant that I did not have a passport to leave Zimbabwe.

When it came time for me to move to Australia, we had to find a way to get my Zimbabwean papers. It started off with my mom and my dad having to go to the capital city in Harare to apply for my Zimbabwean birth certificate. My parents didn't know anything about the process or whether it would be possible. They went to the Registry of Births and Deaths and hoped for the best. When the Zimbabwean government issued me with a Zimbabwean birth certificate, I was able to apply for a passport. That is where I learned another valuable lesson that I have taken with me through life: *I shouldn't wait for everything to line up perfectly in order to pursue my dreams. In the process of pursuing my dreams I can resolve the obstacles.*

A visa to go to Australia is one of the hardest visas in the world to obtain, particularly if you are a Zimbabwean citizen. To obtain my Australian student visa, I had to complete health checks for tuberculosis, have a legal guardian because I was a minor, show proof of funds for my high school fees and reasonable living expenses, which would be thousands of dollars, show I had funds for my flight, and prove where I would be staying in advance. I didn't think much of this at this stage of my life—it was just part of the process. Uncle Andrew was my guarantor for everything as he had promised. In time, I discovered that not all citizenships are equal. British, American, and European nationals did not have to go through the same process I did, which is why Uncle Andrew said we would need to fight. We fought and we won.

**I shouldn't wait for everything to line up perfectly in order to pursue my dreams. In the process of pursuing my dreams I can resolve the obstacles.**

As always, when you go against the grain and try something new, you're going to make enemies. For me, during this time, the enemy was the headmaster of my school in Zimbabwe. He actually said that if I went overseas, I would likely commit suicide. At the time, I allowed that to make me feel stupid and small. Being in a leadership position, he should've been helping me soar, but there will always be someone trying to get in the way of your dream. That is the moment when I started to grow very cautious about who I gave power to in my life. Everyone has an opinion about how I should live, but there are only five people I listen to and take advice from.

At fifteen years old, I learned that to make my dreams come true, I must be my own cheerleader and be prepared to put in the work. My circumstances are not unique to me. I'm a Black, gay, African man. Anything that matters in life requires unquestionable belief in the dream and oneself and a lot of hard work. This could mean marriage or becoming a global superstar, a billionaire, or a world-class athlete. Take it from all the greats who have said it before me: Beyoncé, Simone Biles, Angela Merkel, Michelle Obama, Oprah Winfrey, Viola Davis, Danai Gurira, Lupita Nyong'o, Chimamanda Ngozi Adichie, my mum (Rosemary Gomo), and my grandmother (Mbuya Mutukumira). The moment we declare our dreams will be the moment we are faced with forces and circumstances that will act against our dreams. Often, these forces are other people's fear. Ignore the noise and keep your eye on the prize.

**Anything that matters in life requires unquestionable belief in the dream and oneself and a lot of hard work.**

## When Dreams Meet Reality

Growing up we would hear stories of those who had left to go to the West. There would be a lot of mixed emotions in these families because, when you go overseas, you never really know when you're going to see your children again. There is always this idea that there's a better life wherever you are going and then you have to work hard to create and build something for yourself. At sixteen years old, few people left and ventured off on their own simply because they didn't have the resources and networks to leave Zimbabwe for holiday, let alone for an unknown period of time. Out of one thousand kids in my graduating class, I was probably the only one to leave. It's a rare feat, and there are so many barriers that a Black person must surpass to be able to go to the West. Most Zimbabwe residents will agree that going to the West is the ultimate opportunity for a plethora of reasons. This big move is an escape from poverty and corruption, and it opens doors to education and medical care. It is a quest for safety and human rights. It's such a common dream to leave Zimbabwe but so few end up accomplishing it because they do not have the means to surpass the barriers. I faced these barriers head on, which allowed me to achieve an incredibly rare opportunity.

When I received the email from the Australian High Commission that I had been granted a two-year visa to complete my secondary education in Australia, I was elated and filled with feelings of freedom. I would be the first in my lineage to have accomplished such a feat. I also knew that I would not be coming back to Zimbabwe until I had become successful. Nobody told me this. It was an unspoken agreement. Before I left for the promised land, my parents arranged my goodbye tour, involving visits to my grandmother, aunts, uncles, cousins, and close family friends all around the country.

I don't remember much of this trip, but I do remember saying goodbyes to my grandmother, Mbuya Gomo. She lived in a village with no running water, no electricity, and dry arid soil. My dad, brother, and I eventually dug a well in her homestead that provided her water. Mbuya Gomo hated the city and believed that she belonged to the land. She had no idea of what or where Australia was. When my father explained where I was going, he said, "Remember that time I went to the UK in a vehicle up in the air and you didn't see me for two years?" It was then my grandmother understood that I was going to a far, far away land.

The one person I was unable to say goodbye to was Mbuya Mutukumira, having died of lung cancer when I was fourteen years old. The doctors said her death would've been preventable if it had been caught earlier, but there were few clinics, few hospitals, few medicines, and little access to information in Zimbabwe. Annual health checks were unheard of. My mum, dad, brother, and I nursed her until her death. She died gracefully, without fear, and connected to the notion that she lived life on her own terms. Still, she is with me every day—we laugh, we cry, we smile, we gossip, we plan. She played her part; she passed on the baton to me. I took the baton and forged my own path on the foundations she created.

DREAMS

# CHAPTER 2

# Coming to Australia

## Arriving in Australia

On January 16, 2001, I arrived in Australia. My first stop was Sydney. With one suitcase, a backpack, my passport, and three hundred dollars, I walked through the exit gate with an unwavering smile planted on my face. On the other side waited Uncle Andrew and a twelve-year-old boy named Leigh who he was fostering.

Uncle Andrew arranged for us to stay in Sydney for about three days before heading to my new home in Melbourne. Naturally, I was in awe, as Sydney is a city that people from all around the world come to visit. Getting off the plane was like entering a different universe; nothing like this exists in Mutare.

We arrived in Circular Quay, which is not far from the central business district. There were restaurants everywhere. People from all around the world were walking down the streets: Asians, Middle Easterners, Europeans, South Americans, one or two Black people. I thought Sydney must be the model of universality. Everyone was here, in peace.

Circular Quay is majestic. Circular Quay is home to the Sydney Opera House, the Royal Botanical Gardens, the Sydney Harbor Bridge, and the Sydney Ferry that transports about fifteen million people a year along the Sydney Harbor. There is nothing like it. The Opera House and the Sydney Harbor Bridge together is one of the most famous views in the entire world. The Sydney Harbor is the world's largest and deepest natural harbor, often dotted with massive cruise ships. My adventure had started. It was like being in the *Nancy Drew* novels that I had spent my childhood reading.

Between the jet lag and newness of it all, my first few days in Australia flew by in a blur. I remember catching the ferry on the Sydney Harbor Bridge as the wind whipped my skin. I remember going to McDonald's and seeing the golden arches with my own eyes for the first time. I remember saying "Thank you" to a lady who said, "No worries," back—a response I had never heard before. Coming to Australia was one of the first times I felt safe. I could breathe.

## My New Home

My new home was located in a suburb called Box Hill South in Melbourne. It had four bedrooms—Uncle Andrew's being an ensuite. There was a lounge area with an open kitchen, a second lounge area that was converted into a bedroom, a bathroom with a shower and toilet, and a huge office for Uncle Andrew's business—Tendai Travel—which had its own separate toilet. At the time, five of us were staying at the home as Uncle Andrew was a foster parent looking after three other children/teens/young adults at the time. I had the smallest room in the house. It was meant to be one of those small studies, and I loved it. It had everything I needed: a bed, a chest of draws, a desk, and a night lamp.

Growing up in Zimbabwe, whenever I thought of countries like Australia, Canada, or New Zealand, I imagined them to be an extension of Great Britain and British culture from the books I had read. I was wrong. Many things were different from the books as well as my own upbringing in Zimbabwe. In Australia, people had dedicated internet at home and in school. In Zimbabwe, the little who were able to afford it were still using dial-up internet. In Australia, people had dishwashers for the dishes and washing machines for the laundry. In Zimbabwe, we washed our dishes and clothes by hand. We also had a live-in maid. The maid would be a young woman from a rural area—usually a relative who would stay with us on the provision. She would obtain a skill set in order to live an independent life. In Australia, we practically did everything ourselves. In Australia, houses had ducted heating to cool or heat the home. In Zimbabwe, we used wood fireplaces to keep us warm in the winter and fans to cool our bodies in the summer. In Zimbabwe, dinnertime was with my family—a time to talk about our day at school or at work. In Australia, not everyone had dinner together and it often consisted of families congregated around the TV. In Australia, many homes were made from wood. In Zimbabwe, homes in the city were made from brick. Those who lived in homes made from wood were extremely poor. In Australia, not everyone valued going to school, whereas in Zimbabwe, school was everyone's dream for a better life.

There were a lot of things to adjust to. Initially, I fell into the trap of comparing what was good and what was bad. I have come to learn that many of my initial judgments of good and bad were wrong and that it takes time, sometimes years, to understand the nuances of a new culture.

Living under Uncle Andrew's roof was challenging for me because many of the foster boys had come from troubled homes. Some of them had come from a home where their parents had been drug addicts. Some of them had been kicked out of their home because of their difficult behavior. Some of them had parents who were just incapable of looking after them. There were few values that we shared. Some of the boys would play loud music in the middle of the night; sometimes, they would yell at Uncle Andrew. It is unfathomable for a child to yell back at an adult in Zimbabwe—especially your mom and dad. Some of the boys would refuse to do their chores, something that would never happen in my home. When given chores, they are done to the highest standard.

I didn't leave Zimbabwe because I came from a broken home. My home was filled with love. I left Zimbabwe because of the opportunities I wanted to seize, which were very different to what Zimbabwe could offer me. I am often asked if I became homesick. The simple answer is no. I never allowed myself to feel that way. I told myself being homesick was a waste of time as that would hold me back from accomplishing my dream. I was razor-sharp focused on creating my new life in the West. Unbeknownst to me, denying these feelings would lead to excruciating pain later in life.

Despite my challenging living conditions, to this day, I am very grateful for living with those boys because they taught me so much about life. Who they've become today despite the obstacles in their childhood inspires me and fills my heart with joy. One of them runs his own cement business. One of them is married with two kids and has his own property investments. Uncle Andrew created a space for all of us to have an opportunity to have a life greater than the one we were born into.

## My Time at Kingswood College

In Zimbabwe, your quality of life was determined by how much you followed the well-trodden path. This path was the insurance of getting a good-paying job, a good spouse, a good group of friends, a good social club. The problem with the well-trodden path is that it doesn't guarantee happiness. Coming to Australia did not mean I would be happy. I still held onto beliefs about who I should be in many areas of my life. Kingswood College taught me to examine whether I would blindly follow the well-trodden path or examine who I wanted to be in different contexts of my life. I had to make decisions around my view of myself, my education, my religion, my social groups, my hobbies, and even the clothes I wore. This was not easy.

I remember my first day of school. I was excited and nervous. I had no idea what I was going to be walking into when I came to school. When I arrived, there was this sea of white faces and some Asian faces. I was the only Black person. The school administrator took me to my classroom, and I could feel everyone looking at me. *Do they know that I'm not wealthy like them? What do they know about my life circumstances? Do they think that I'm a charity case?* Here I was, living my dream while being held hostage to negative thoughts.

I entered the classroom and immediately felt like I stuck out like a sore thumb. My chocolate-brown skin gave me away. I sat down, and as everybody else was already settled, some students came to talk to me, and my heart started racing because I had no idea what was now going to happen next. The students were very nice. They welcomed me to the school. They made themselves available for any questions that I may have. Over time, I came to realize that Kingswood College was a very special school—welcoming, inclusive, pioneering, creative. The people I met at Kingswood were instrumental in forging my path. I thought it would be my books and grades that would be my education, but it was actually the friends and community I found at Kingswood College.

## Black Is Beautiful

On my first day of school, a classmate and I were walking into our biology class. She was beautiful. As we were walking, she turned to me and said, "I've always wanted to marry a Black person. Your skin is so beautiful." I was so shocked. Not once had I ever thought of myself as beautiful and yet here I was, hearing it from a white person. Growing up in Zimbabwe, many of the white Zimbabweans made us feel that white was better than Black. Imagine that story being told for over one hundred years to an entire continent. Many Black people in the world today wake up in the morning with low self-esteem because they are Black, something that they have no control over. I haven't met any white person in my life who has discussed low self-esteem because of their skin color. However, among the people I meet from Asia, the Middle East, and South America during my travels, there is a conversation of unworthiness and low self-esteem because of the color of their skin. To come to Australia and hear a white person say they would like to have Black babies was mind blowing because, up until that point, I was not walking this earth telling myself that Black is beautiful. In Australia, I discovered that I am beautiful.

## Learning to Forget Rote Learning

Growing up in Zimbabwe, you experienced a very traditional way of learning. You learned by rote. When you read textbooks, you applied the learnings exactly as they say. When you're taught by a teacher, you apply the lesson exactly the way it was expressed. Thinking outside how the teacher taught or what the textbook said was not encouraged. Conversely, in my last two years of high school in Australia, the teachers wanted to know what I thought about history, world affairs, and the books I read. I was so used to being spoon-fed, being told what to think and how to think about it. My last two years of high school taught me to think for myself and this was very hard.

## Subject Selection

In Zimbabwe, there is a specific combination of school subjects you must take in order to successfully be accepted for certain university programs. For example, if you wanted to become a lawyer, you had to study English literature, geography, and history. If you wanted to practice medicine, you had to study math, physics, and chemistry. You couldn't study English literature, math, and physics and enter medical school. As a sixteen-year-old, I wanted to keep my options open. I had no idea what career I wanted at such an age. In Australia, there are still prerequisites to enter into law or medicine, but the variety of subjects I could take allowed me to keep my options open. I studied legal studies, English, math, chemistry, biology, and university-level biology. I could apply for careers in humanities, sciences, or both. Everything was available to me.

## Religion and Spirituality

I learned that my value system was very different than other peoples' value systems. In Zimbabwe, most people are Christian and nearly everyone goes to church, including myself. In Australia, none of my friends at school believed in God nor did they go to church. Not going to church on Sundays was taboo to me. I continued to go to church while in Australia, and over time, my thinking changed about religion and spirituality. I didn't know that non-Christians could be kind, generous, and loving. I learned that Christianity did not have a monopoly on love. I had to face the fact that Jews are loving, Hindus are loving, Muslims are loving, agnostics are loving, and atheists are loving. I came to understand that love exists in all people irrespective of their belief system. What would being a Christian mean to me if good and bad things can be found in all belief systems? What would be my path now?

## Parties

Another thing that came as a surprise to me was the party culture in Australia. I was shocked to see people drinking alcohol and smoking. Growing up as a teenager in Zimbabwe, none of my friends drank or smoked. People who drank alcohol were typically considered "losers" and lived in the shantytowns. They were not the kind of people I wanted to hang around with if I wanted to be successful in life. In Australia, getting drunk—or, as they say, "getting wasted"—was acceptable behavior, even a badge of honor. In Zimbabwe, getting drunk is a failure not just on the person who gets intoxicated but on the entire family for failing to instill the value of self-control.

## Stepping Out of My Comfort Zone

At Kingswood College, everything was possible. I remember my friend Steve Coles asking me if I was going to audition for the school's performance of Andrew Lloyd Webber's musical *Jesus Christ Superstar*. I told him I was interested but wasn't going to do it. However, he convinced me to audition, and I got the role of Simon. This opportunity allowed me to meet many of the kids from years seven to twelve. I made new friends with whom, little did I know, would be instrumental in my next phase of life.

This was not the first time Steve made me do things out of my comfort zone. His friendship ensured that I broke out of my shell and tried the things I would never have considered doing in Zimbabwe. Steve made me try out for the basketball team (which I failed). Steve made me attend Friday pizza night when I wanted to stay home and study. I made new friends. Steve fixed Uncle Andrew's car when I scratched it. He saved my bacon. Steve was the constant voice who insisted I try, even if I was unsure if I would be good at it or even like it. We all need people like Steve in our lives, people who support and lift us up.

## Stepping Out of the Uniform

In Zimbabwe, from the time I was six until I was sixteen, I spent most of my life in khakis. Khaki was the color of our school uniform. At Kingswood College, we did not have to wear a uniform for the last two years of high school. We were taught to choose and be responsible with what we wear. I was scared. I had never really thought about what I would want to wear on my own terms. Shaun, who was one of the men who boarded with Uncle Andrew, took me clothes shopping. We went to this big warehouse called the Direct Factory Outlet (DFO). We had nothing like that in my small city in Mutare. We passed a shop that had some bright-colored clothes, but I couldn't allow myself to try them on. I already stood out being the only Black man in most spaces. I told myself that I would stand out even more if I dared to wear colorful clothing. Shaun noticed my interest in the clothes and encouraged me to try them. I tried on a bright orange top. It was tight-fitting and hugged my body perfectly. I'd never worn anything like it and I had no idea that clothing could make me feel so good. Prior to this moment, I had mostly worn box T-shirts, so I loved the tight fit of this shirt. I bought it. If I could, I would have worn it every day. It would be easy to wear clothes that made me blend in with others, but I have learned that what I wear gives myself and others the confidence to be our unique, whole, and complete selves.

> **I learned that there is wisdom in all paths, but my job is to take the wisdom that is right for me and discard the rest.**

Coming to Australia taught me that the well-trodden path may not be my path. There is no formula to life. I learned that there is wisdom in all paths, but my job is to take the wisdom that is right for me and discard the rest. If I can't find any wisdom in any of the paths, I can forge my own.

## My Job at McDonald's

I needed money to support myself in Australia. In Zimbabwe, you don't look for a job until you finish university because there is simply no time to work. Life is dedicated to studying. Then, once you make it to university, you continue studying day and night to get a professional job. This means that doing anything other than study is jeopardizing your chances of a great career. Your grades are a measure of your worth and opportunity. In Australia, there are some similarities with wanting to achieve good grades, but your grades don't limit your opportunities.

In Australia, it is a rite of passage to start working when you turn fifteen years and nine months old. Because I was sixteen, Uncle Andrew encouraged me to apply for a job at McDonald's as it had a good training program. We didn't have a McDonald's in Zimbabwe in 2001, but many of us had heard of it. Entering a new country, McDonald's was like a symbol of progress, stability, and success. With fear and enthusiasm, I went to four different McDonald's close to my home to seek a job.

My first interview was with the McDonald's in Blackburn South. The interview seemed to be going well and I could answer all the questions with confidence. At one point, they asked me what my dreams were. I told them that after I finished high school, I wanted to go to Oxford University in the United Kingdom. I didn't get the job.

In my debrief with Uncle Andrew, he discouraged me from telling the interviewers those kinds of dreams. My next interview was at the McDonald's at Box Hill Central. The interviewer asked me why I wanted to work there. I told him that McDonald's did not exist in Zimbabwe, but that my mum had been to McDonald's when she was on a work trip in Vancouver, and she liked it. He gave me the job on the spot and assigned me to the Box Hill North location. I was thrilled. After accepting the job, the next step was determining whether I wanted to work in the kitchen—or as Uncle Andrew calls it, being the "burger flipper"—or the front counter taking people's orders. I knew immediately I wanted to work at the front counter. Little did I know that at the time, male employees worked in the kitchen and females worked at the front counter. I later found out that I was the only one given the option. Today, I'm still not sure why. Just like my mum and dad had taught me, there is no such thing as boy or girl jobs. There are just jobs and boys and girls can do anything.

It had taken me about three months to find a job after I arrived in Australia. Uncle Andrew was proud of me. I was proud of me. Having a job allowed me to have more independence in my life. Uncle Andrew stopped paying me an allowance of ten dollars. The money

I earned from work was to be used for necessities like clothes, books for school, public transport, and emergencies. Uncle Andrew was responsible for my accommodations, food, and my school fees. I spent my money frugally. Every other cent was to be saved in preparation for my next opportunity. It was my responsibility to have the resources for what came next in my future.

I remember my training at McDonald's. I thought everything was so professionally done. They gave us this little book with all the ingredients and the nutritional value of the food that we offered. In the book, it said that the chips had different types of vitamin B. I never knew potatoes had vitamins and I couldn't wait to go home and tell Uncle Andrew how healthy the chips were at McDonald's. I remember Uncle Andrew looking at me skeptically as I showed him the book that detailed these nutritional facts.

I loved working at McDonald's. I was working in a multinational organization that had a good training program, a great system, and *nutritional food*. For me, it was like working for a five-star restaurant at that time in my life. I would always get to work early. I would make sure that all the tables were sparkling clean. When a customer walked through the front doors of the store, I would ensure I was at the till before they stepped in front of it, and I'd welcome each and every person with a beaming smile. I made it my job to make others feel welcomed and I looked after the restaurant as if it were my own.

I dreaded the three o'clock rush when the tradespeople would come in after work. For about two weeks, I couldn't understand what they were saying. At times, I even doubted we were even speaking the same language. They talked fast with a broad accent. The way I used English was different to them. I remember one of the tradies saying, "I'd like a couple of cheeseburgers." When I asked him how many, he responded, "A couple." I was puzzled. I didn't know why he wasn't answering my question. I asked again, "How many cheeseburgers?" Once again, he said, "A couple." He was getting frustrated. I was getting nervous. I couldn't understand why he wasn't answering my question. I tried to think why he kept responding with "a couple." It dawned on me that "a couple" could mean two. I gave him two cheeseburgers hoping I was right, and I was. Growing up in Zimbabwe, "a couple" meant "many."

My coworkers and I did not see eye to eye. They did not take their job at McDonald's seriously. They were sloppy. They didn't do their hair properly. They didn't wear their uniforms with pride. In my head, I was screaming, "Don't you know you've got this opportunity to work in this top restaurant? You're not giving it the respect it deserves." I felt separate from most of my coworkers. I felt lonely because I judged them, and they judged me. I think the other coworkers didn't want me to be working very hard because it looked like I was trying to be better than them. If I am being paid to do a service, I will do it to the best of my ability. To me, it was like theft to not do a job I have been paid to do.

I loved my customers, and they loved me. There was the Filet-O-Fish lady who would come through the drive-thru with her dark glasses and order me around like she was the queen. I adored her. There was the middle-aged brother and sister who would sit outside with their coffee and limitless refills, while they chain-smoked and read the newspaper for hours. I loved them. There was John, the elderly man who would come in and talk my ear off about everything. I loved him. This was my community. Everyone was welcomed, just like my mum and dad had taught me. I would get tips from my customers. The managers of McDonald's were perplexed. Nothing like this had ever happened. Nobody got tips at McDonald's. I got promoted very quickly due to my work ethic and became the youngest assistant shift manager at the store.

This new role meant that I was responsible for running the entire store during my shift. I was responsible for stock take, rosters, covering shifts when people called in sick, the cleanliness of the store and the toilets, ensuring that we were operating as one team, and preparing the tills for the next shift manager. At only nineteen years old, I had learned everything about how to run a store, but bigger responsibilities come with more challenges.

My biggest challenge at McDonald's showed up not long after I became the assistant shift manager. I discovered that money was missing from the tills. The managers lied to the owner regarding how much money there was because they were scared they would be fired. They asked me to conspire with them and keep their secret. I felt trapped. Keep the secret and fit in with the managers or tell the truth and risk something bad happening to me? "I could be arrested for theft and deported," I thought to myself. I decided to find a way to tell the owner of the store. I waited for a day when all the managers were not working, and I asked to speak with him privately. When I told him that the money in the tills did not match up, he thanked me and immediately went to his office to count the cash.

A few days later, the owner called a management meeting and said that when he was taking inventory, he discovered there was a bit of money missing from the tills. When he asked us what happened, everyone remained silent until the store manager Ben broke the silence and attempted to say some words. But in the end, the owner just said he had replaced the cash, and it would be our responsibility to make sure that the money doesn't go missing and to immediately inform him if it did. I could feel a wave of relief crash over the room. No one got in trouble. No one got fired. Nobody found out that I was the one who brought this lie to light. Speaking up was a gift for me and the managers. I was free. We were all free. I learned that my integrity, my peace of mind, and standing for my values is more valuable than being liked and part of the in crowd.

I am a whistleblower. I completely understand why we need to protect people who do the right thing like Frank Serpico, Edward Snowden, and Chelsea Manning. When I was completing my third year of high school in Zimbabwe, a teacher had beaten up a student with a belt on his buttocks. (While I don't believe it is right, corporal punishment in Zimbabwe was normal.) In this particular case, the teacher went too far, shredding my friend Tinotenda Shumba's skin. I was outraged. My entire class was outraged. I started a petition to have this teacher removed

**I learned that my integrity, my peace of mind, and standing for my values is more valuable than being liked and part of the in crowd.**

from the school. I typed a letter to give to the Ministry of Education and I got every student in my class to sign it. The students of the class next door also signed my petition.

The following day, three of us were pulled out of class and summoned. The teacher who had brutally beaten up Tinotenda had gotten a whiff of my ploy. A fellow student had betrayed us. This teacher considered the three of us as ring leaders and threatened us by saying if we were to move forward with the petition, he would ensure that our other teachers would punish us by giving us low grades. In short, lower grades meant our chances to progress to the fourth year of high school would be hindered. When we got back to our classroom, we debated the situation with our classmates. The other two ringleaders backed down and requested that I didn't send the petition to the

Ministry of Education. I still had my typed letter and all the signatures with me. I walked to the Ministry of Education, defying the request of my classmates. When I reached the door, I stood still and turned back.

For many years following this incident, I regretted letting the bully win, and it still stings me today that I let fear rule me. I promised myself to *never* sell out on what matters to me again. Martin Luther King Jr. never sold out, Nelson Mandela never sold out, Rosa Parks never sold out, and Malaya Yousafzai never sold out. What will you stand for?

## The World Is My Teacher

My education continued outside the classroom. After my first year in Australia, Uncle Andrew took me overseas. We went to Thailand, England, Scotland, France, and Israel. There is no greater education than traveling the world and interacting with people from all walks of life.

In Thailand, I got to join a group of Western Australians doing voluntary work. We stayed with the Lau villagers up in the mountains, helping to build schools and teach English. Many Thai people in this village had never seen a Black person before. The kids in the village feared me. Every time I approached them, they ran away. In life, we tend to be afraid of what we don't know, what we don't understand. I know what it is to be afraid of what I don't understand. I did not take their fear of me personally.

**In life, we tend to be afraid of what we don't know, what we don't understand. I know what it is to be afraid of what I don't understand.**

Going to the United Kingdom was very special to me. I have no memories of my birth country, so it was a big adventure. As I am a huge *Harry Potter* fan, one of our stops was to Kings Cross Station to see Platform 9 ¾, the fictional portal to Hogwarts. We also visited Oxford University—my dream school. I spent a lot of time browsing the huge bookshops and contemplating how many thinkers who shaped the world were educated in this exact location.

We celebrated Christmas in Scotland in Aberfeldy with Uncle Andrew's friends. It was extremely cold. I attempted to ski for the first time in my life. I fell a lot and felt cold. I did not fall in love with skiing. One of our last stops was the town of my birth. We visited Aunty Margaret, who took care of my parents in the eighties and still lived in Ipswich in Norfolk. I got to see the hospital I was born in—Norwich Hospital—before it was closed permanently and later demolished. After my sojourn to the United Kingdom, I knew I never wanted to live in Great Britain. It was cold, wet, and gets dark at 3:00 p.m. in the winter. It also seemed as if everyone was in a bad mood because they had to work multiple jobs to survive because of the cost of living. This alone made me appreciate the quality of life that I had in Australia.

> I am hopeful this is possible for the future. A peaceful, harmonious, and loving world.

We visited Jerusalem, which is still one of my favorite cities in the world. The historic city is beautiful, bustling with people and smelling like delicious food everywhere. The narrow streets and high walls are filled with people selling their wares. To see what existed over two millennia ago and to hear the stories of the past being told with passion, as if the events happened yesterday, was a spiritual experience. To hear about the pain, suffering, and hope experienced in one place was humbling. What I loved most was how Jerusalem is a space for Jews, Muslims, Christians, and Armenians, and all people are welcome to visit. That is how the world should be—inclusive to all people and all religions living in harmony. This may not be how the world is today, but I am hopeful this is possible for the future. A peaceful, harmonious, and loving world.

## We Are All the Same

Anything that demonizes any part of humanity makes no sense to me. To me, we are all part of humanity. I haven't had the opportunity to interview every single person on earth, but it seems to me that we all bleed; we all have fears; we all have dreams irrespective of gender, sex, nationality, culture, religion, and sexual orientation. I choose to walk this earth seeking similarities between myself and others, straying away from fixating on the differences. Living my life in the context of why the other person is not the same as me keeps me separate and isolated from them and from myself. Separation is the breeding ground for fear, mistrust, and hatred, which leads to racism; misogyny; homophobia; and the entitlement to kill, start wars, and even commit genocide.

**Separation is the breeding ground for fear, mistrust, and hatred, which leads to racism, misogyny, homophobia, and the entitlement to kill, start wars, and even genocide.**

Traveling the world was very different from the stories I read in books. I got to talk to people, smell the places, experience the weather, soak in the culture, eat the local food, make friends, and ask questions. While traveling, I learned that the world is more loving, inclusive, and empathetic than I thought it was. I value experiential learning as it built my empathy and compassion, as well as allowing me to find love.

# CHAPTER 3

## Surpassing Fear and Uncertainty

At Kingswood College, I made some great friends and won the Legal Studies award two years in a row. I was elected as Sports Captain in my last year of high school. I performed in *Jesus Christ Superstar*. I successfully completed year twelve biology in year eleven, and I had been accepted into an exclusive program at the University of Melbourne to study biology while I was only still in year twelve. They only accepted about twenty students throughout the state of Victoria. My life was full. I was studying like crazy, working as much as I could at McDonald's to save money for my next opportunity, attending extra classes, going to church, and maintaining a social life. It was a lot.

My time at Kingswood College was coming to an end. What should have been a time of possibility and excitement for me was plagued with fear and uncertainty. There were so many barriers in order to continue my journey for a better life. At this point, I was eighteen and I had decided that I wanted to go to university and study law, but my options were bleak. I decided on law because I thought a law degree would allow me to help people and provide me with opportunities in both Australia and the entire world. I thought that having a law degree would give me power.

Uncle Andrew always said that he would only support me for two years. He did not want me to stay in Australia because he believed I would be corrupted by the materialistic culture. He wanted me to return to Zimbabwe after my high school education, but I had other plans. Even if he wanted to support me, Uncle Andrew did not have the financial resources for my university, fees which would be between $12,000 and $20,000 per year for an international student. I had no ill will toward Uncle Andrew. He had always been upfront about his commitments to me, and he gave me a new experience beyond what I could have imagined for myself as the boy from a little-known town.

Returning to Zimbabwe was not an option for me for numerous reasons. Growing up, Zimbabwe was considered the breadbasket of Africa. While it used to have enough food to feed its neighboring countries, it all changed just before I left. You see, Zimbabwe was one of the last countries in the world to be decolonized. The situation is complex, but my understanding is that there was an agreement called the Lancaster Agreement in 1979 between the United Kingdom and Zimbabwe, brokered by the Americans that permitted the white farmers who were the descendants of the British to retain land for twenty years after Zimbabwean independence. Afterward, there would be a buyback scheme funded by the United Kingdom, which was to take place in the year 2000, twenty years after independence. White Zimbabweans constituted less than 1 percent of the population, yet they owned about 70 percent of the arable land of the whole country.

The Zimbabwe government could not keep its commitments because it had used the funds for the buybacks for their own personal gain. Many people who fought for independence lived in abject poverty and they were rightly demanding change. In the government's fight to retain its power, it pointed the finger at the white Zimbabweans and encouraged the former war veterans and everyone who was disenfranchised to invade white-owned farms. And they did. This led to the destruction of Zimbabwe. There was no food in the shops, there was no petrol … the Zimbabwean dollar became worthless. My parents lost everything.

I had never grown up with violence, but the news cycles all around the world were about the violence in Zimbabwe. It didn't just target white farmers. It targeted anyone who opposed the government. This is when Zimbabwe fell into a dictatorship. As I was outwardly living my "best life" in Australia, I was having to compartmentalize what was happening in Zimbabwe. Would my mum, dad, sister, and brother be killed? I avoided the news. I couldn't bear the thought of my family being murdered. I would fall apart, which would impact my studies, resulting in me having to return to Zimbabwe to nothing. I blocked out what was happening in my home country and focused on the task at hand: my education. Going back to Zimbabwe was not an option. That door was firmly closed, but those unprocessed feelings would betray me later.

## The Importance of Sharing Your Story

While walking to one of my classes, I ran into Principal Bennett. She brought up the conversation of university to me, asking me where I planned on going. I felt ashamed that I had no money and no plan, but I shared my thoughts with her anyway. We both stopped walking. She asked me, "Would it be okay if I shared your story in the school newsletter? Maybe some of the parents in the community may want to support you." I had a decision to make in that moment. To say yes and have everyone know my story or to say no and keep it hidden. I debated not saying yes because I had already been a burden to so many people, but I said yes anyway.

The newsletter was published, sharing all my hopes and dreams. Putting it out there for hundreds of parents and students to see was frightening. I kept asking myself whether I was worthy enough to be helped in this way, and I felt the same way I felt when I debated asking Uncle Andrew for help. History was repeating itself.

Several days later, I was called into Principal Bennett's office. There was a white lady with thick black hair sitting in one of the chairs. She sounded a touch British. Mrs. Bennett introduced her to me as Mrs. Kennedy. Mrs. Kennedy was the mother of one of my friends and she had read the newsletter and wanted to help. She had a special connection to my story. She had lived in Zimbabwe and empathized with my circumstances. She took on being my ambassador to ensure I found a way to stay in Australia. Mrs. Kennedy helped me bring my dreams to life; she was my voice, she was the action taker, and she found a way to overcome obstacles.

## The Roller Coaster of Failure

The day had arrived. My two years in Australia culminated to this moment, obtaining my high school results. In Victoria, the highest Australian Tertiary Admission Rank (ATAR score) you can obtain when completing high school is 99.99. I opened my results. My score was 92.65. I was in the top 8 percent of the state. I had performed exceedingly well but I was disappointed.

Getting into law school immediately after high school in Australia is very hard. I wanted to stay in Melbourne, as this is where I had built my community. There were only two law schools that were consistently recommended to me: Melbourne Law School and Monash Law School. My ATAR score was not good enough to be offered a place to study at Melbourne or Monash Law School. I had failed.

Everyone was celebrating my success. I joined in the celebration but internally I was not happy. I chastised myself for not working hard enough. When I got my results, Mrs. Kennedy asked me what I wanted to study at university. I told her I wanted to study law. I had been offered a place to study law at Deakin University, but my heart had been set on Melbourne or Monash Law School. I had missed out on Monash by 2.35 points on the ATAR exam, and Melbourne by a little more. I had given up on this dream. But Mrs. Kennedy had other ideas. She decided that we were going to go directly to Monash University to see if we could talk them into giving me a place to study law, as I had barely missed the mark. I thought this was absurd, but I followed her lead.

Mrs. Kennedy and I went directly to the admissions office at Monash University, where they reaffirmed that my scores were too low. However, there hadn't been many international students apply to study law so there were spots available. She offered me a spot right then and there. I was shocked. This couldn't be happening to me. I now had options—Deakin University or Monash University. But there was yet another obstacle I'd need to surpass: the fees.

Mrs. Kennedy went on to explain my family circumstances and asked if scholarships were available for me, but the admissions officer explained that there were no scholarships for undergraduate degrees for international students to study law. My heart sank.

## Facing the Impossible, Scary Roads

In most universities in Australia, you could go straight into law school from high school unlike in the United States where law school is a graduate degree. However, to undertake law school right after high school, you had to do a double degree concurrently. There were numerous combinations you could do. You could study law/biomedical science, law/commerce, law/arts. I opted to study a double degree in arts and law. I chose an arts degree as I believed it would give me context to history, economics, and politics, which would make me a more well-rounded human being. My double degree would take five years to complete.

Even though my heart was set on going to Monash University, I had to check my ego and look at what was doable. The school fees for Deakin University were $12,000 per year. At Monash University, my first year alone was going to cost over $14,000 in just fees, let alone the books and living expenses. In subsequent years, the fees would spike to $20,000 to $25,000 a year. The school fees alone to complete my double degree at Monash University would be around $120,000. My dream to attend university in Australia seemed impossible.

At eighteen years old, I was having to decide whether I wanted to take on the responsibility of having to pay thousands of dollars for an education. There was no money coming from my parents and I didn't have access to loans. All I had was a couple thousand dollars to my name and an offer to attend law school at universities I couldn't afford. I was at a crossroads.

It seems to me for most people, the ultimate decision whether to do something is based on money—a decision we are faced with every day. Caged eggs for four dollars or free-range eggs for seven dollars? There is a lot of wisdom out there when it comes to being cautious with one's money, but for me, money is not the determinative decision. Money is only one among a myriad of factors. I decided I would go to Monash University even though I had no money to pay for it. My justification was that if I went to Monash, I would create influential relationships that would benefit my life and a degree from that university would open opportunities around the world. I wasn't thinking about today; I was thinking about the rest of my life. I called Mrs. Kennedy and told her that I wanted to accept the offer to go to Monash even though I didn't have the financial means to attend. I felt scared.

## Was I Worthy Enough?

Mrs. Kennedy used her influence to raise money for my university fees. She arranged a dinner at one of the few Ethiopian restaurants in Melbourne and invited people from the Kingswood community to attend. Parents, teachers, and friends of parents came. As I arrived, my heart was racing because my future was going to be determined by the forty smiling people in the room. I was only an eighteen-year-old Black boy among a sea of white faces.

**I was only an eighteen-year-old Black boy among a sea of white faces.**

Most of these people were strangers and there I was asking them to contribute thousands of dollars so that I could have a future in Australia. Would they see me as good enough? Was I worthy enough?

That whole night was a blur. I remember Mrs. Kennedy sharing my story, the circumstances in Zimbabwe, and a sheet of paper was passed along where people got to write their names and their commitment. That night, people donated over $14,000 so that I, Rugare Gomo, could go to university. I was profoundly shocked, paralyzed with gratitude, and moved beyond words. Little me from Mutare,

Zimbabwe, a place most people have never heard of, was again going to have another opportunity to fulfill his dreams.

We had raised the funds for my first year of law school, but I still had one more obstacle: my visa. I had come to Australia on a two-year visa. It was a visa that allowed me to finish high school, and I now needed to get a new one that would allow me to go to university for the next five years.

## Opportunity in My Hands

By the time I had completed high school in 2002, the situation in Zimbabwe had dramatically changed. There was no food in the country. There were long queues for fuel. The University of Zimbabwe had closed, the white commercial farms were now being invaded, and several white farmers were being killed. Anyone who opposed the government was being detained or killed, while others simply disappeared. There was now an influx of Zimbabwean refugees in Australia, New Zealand, Great Britain, the United States, and neighboring African countries. What that meant was that Zimbabwe citizens were deemed a high risk of overstaying their visas.

In 2002, the Australian government ranked countries from "safe," like America and the United Kingdom (Category 1), to war-torn countries like Afghanistan (Category 5). When I applied for my high school visa, Zimbabwe was a Category 2 country. When it was time to apply for my university visa, Zimbabwe was deemed a Category 4 country. Simply put, the visa requirements were onerous for a Zimbabwean national. I would have to show that I had been offered a place for university. Check. I would need to show I am in good health. Check. I would need to show I had money to pay the fees for my first year of university. Check. I would need to show funds for living expenses around $15,000. Fail. Where was I going to get the funds to show the Australian government that I could support myself?

A member of the Kingswood community came to my rescue. Mrs. D'Souza had heard my story. She was a migrant herself from Singapore and an Australian qualified lawyer. She felt connected to my story, and she offered me to move in with her family while I attended university. She would cover all my living expenses as well as pay part of my school fees. I accepted her proposal.

When I had my paperwork in order, I applied for my visa. Several weeks later, I got an email confirming that my visa was granted. My heart was filled with joy. I had an additional five years to forge my own path.

Creating the opportunity to attend university was hard and likely would've never happened if the people and situations didn't arrive in my life when they did. I didn't get the right ATAR score, I didn't have the funds to go to university, I had no money for my living expenses. Yet, in my hands, I held my passport with my most precious asset: a five-year Australian visa, which permitted me to pursue an arts and law degree. I was determined to make the most of this opportunity.

When I look at my life today, I am often astounded that the people in it would never be here had I not been uncompromising about who I wanted to be and what I wanted to accomplish. When I had no voice, a stranger spoke for me. When I had no hope, a stranger held hope for me. When I had low self-esteem, a stranger built me up. When the doors where closed shut, a stranger opened a door for me. I did not get to choose my community. Strangers chose me. They became my community. The one thing in common all these strangers have is empathy. Empathy is the energy that created the path I have today. To you, stranger, I am eternally grateful.

DREAMS

CHAPTER 4

# Making the Most of the Opportunities in My Path

When my first day at university came, I was beyond excited. I had worked hard all summer at McDonald's to save money for my books and living expenses. I felt empowered to go into my first semester with sustainable funds. A few weeks before university started, Mrs. Kennedy and I went to Monash University to choose my subjects for both my Bachelor of Arts and Bachelor of Law degrees. There were so many options that it was difficult to choose. I reminded myself of my goal: to be able to obtain global opportunities. For my arts degree, I chose to do a double major in French and European Studies. My choices were specific and intentional. Other than English, French is the most common language in many international organizations. I chose European Studies because I wanted to understand why we lived in a Eurocentric world. For my law degree, I had to complete the Priestly 11 Subjects, which are required to be admitted as a lawyer. I would not be eligible to pick up any electives until my third year.

Later, I decided to do an honors year in my arts degrees. This added an extra year to my time at university, totaling six years.

On my first day of law school, I was excited and overwhelmed, knowing that I was sitting in the same class as some of the brightest minds in the country. When the professor walked into the room at nine o'clock sharp, I was shocked. He was Black. His name was Professor Emanuel Laryea, and he was one of the few Black people I had met since I'd been in Australia over the past two years. While it was rare to be around other Black people, it was even more rare to be in the presence of a Black professional. So, as you can imagine, discovering that my first professor was Black came as quite a shock to me. For the first time in Australia, I was no longer the only Black person in the room. During my six years at Monash Law, there was a total of three Black students.

When I went to university, I was the only student from Kingswood College doing law while all my friends were studying elsewhere. I was alone. I was in a new environment with no community. When people would invite me to socialize, I would typically say I was unavailable because I had to go to my next shift at McDonald's to maintain funds for school and living expenses. In my first year, it was hard making friends because, not only did I have to study to keep up, I also had the extra challenge of having to raise my next $20,000 to get into my second year. Every morning, I would get on the bus at 7:30 a.m., study on the commute, attend classes all day, then catch the 3:00 p.m. bus home. From there, I'd take my bike to McDonald's and work an eight-hour shift, riding my bike back home after midnight. Most law students didn't have to deal with that.

My time at university was very hard. I was exhausted all the time and would sometimes fall asleep in class. Everything was in conflict. I needed work for funds for university. I needed sleep to stay awake in class. I needed more time to study and get good grades. Everything was out of harmony, and nothing was in flow. I felt as if everything was working against me. There was no time to feel my feelings; there was no time to process the magnitude of what I was taking on. This is what I had to do to survive. There were no other options. For me, the world had given me everything, and the only feeling I allowed myself to feel was gratitude, peppered with thoughts that "life could be worse." And it was worse for those who had remained in Zimbabwe.

## Deciding What Is Not an Option for Me

I am not an extrovert. I am deeply introverted. I like my own company. I like working on my own projects. I am often mistaken to being extroverted because I love talking in depth about my projects with anyone who will listen. I also like to win at whatever I put my mind to. I was losing the money game for university. If I did not raise the money, I would be deported back to Zimbabwe. This was not an option for me.

I had kept all the names, emails, and phone numbers of the people who contributed toward my school fees. This would be my starting point to continue raising money for university. While asking myself what a donor would want to know about me for them to continue contributing funds, I realized I should actively be participating in the community.

I joined several clubs at Monash University. I didn't want to, but this is what I thought would be a good demonstration of participating in the community. In my first year, I joined Amnesty International. We arranged campaigns and petitions for whatever international catastrophe was happening. In my second year, I was elected by the law students as the Social Justice Officer. I was responsible for arranging events for students to learn about social justice organizations in Australia and around the world, as well as arrange events where students learned about career opportunities outside of top-tier law firms. I also founded Zimbabweaware. The purpose of Zimbabweaware was to engage law students to write to their federal member of parliament to lobby the Australian government to do something about the Zimbabwean crisis.

I wrote a biannual newsletter to everyone on my email list. The newsletter was my way of keeping in touch with my community as well as asking for help. However, I dreaded the thought of people reading the newsletters. It made me feel like I was being evaluated to see if my story would be worthy enough. But I was desperate, so I continued sending them. They always paid off—not just monetarily but also by reminding me of the love I have in my community.

The group that continued to support me the most during my time at university was my Kingswood community. There were so many families who contributed money—from $20 to $5,000. Every cent mattered. My biggest financial supporter was the Chomley family. Each year, they deposited $5,000 into my bank account, no questions asked. I didn't have to prove anything to receive their donation. They contributed about $30,000 over six years. When I got bad grades, they still supported me. I was not a tax-deductible entity, and they still supported me. There were no criteria I had to meet to gain their support. They taught me that doing good has no conditions.

My university fees kept increasing every year. In 2003, my school fees were $14,000, and by 2007, they reached about $25,000. The amount I needed to complete my degrees became harder and harder. I couldn't keep up. One year, I didn't have the $7,000 for the semester. I was desperate. I asked my brother for help. At this time, my brother had managed to get out of Zimbabwe. He had been working for Deloitte & Touche. During the Zimbabwean crisis, Deloitte & Touche UK employed those who wanted to get out of Zimbabwe.

My brother was poor. He was in a new country, and he wasn't making much money. He was overworking to create his own path in life. He had recently married and was supporting himself and his new wife. I was desperate and ashamed of asking for money from him because I already knew how hard it was for him. He sold his car to raise my school fees. He saved what little he had to come up with the $7,000. I asked for an extension from Monash University, and they granted it to me. It was a close call. This was one of the most stressful experiences of my life. To fail to pay my school fees would mean being deported to Zimbabwe. This was not an option for me.

The rest of my money came from working. I worked nonstop, begging for double shifts at McDonald's. On holidays, I would wake up at 4:45 a.m. to go to work. I'd work until 2:00 p.m., take a two-hour break, and then start another shift from 4:00 p.m. until close. Afterward, I would ride my bike home and drive the car to my cleaning job. I would clean offices for two to four hours a couple of nights a week. I worked and worked and worked. I wonder if this is what it was like for my grandmother creating the opportunity for my mum to go to school. She worked and worked and worked. I wonder if this was what it was like for my mum creating opportunities for all her three children. She worked and worked and worked.

**I became many things, but what I cherish the most is that I became able to see people's greatness in all things.**

Raising over $120,000 just for my university fees was hard. It transformed me into a person I never imagined myself to be. I became an activist through Amnesty International and Zimbabweaware. I became a fundraiser and communications expert through my newsletters. I became a leader by being elected the Social Justice Officer in law school. I became a negotiator when I wasn't going to meet my deadlines for payment of fees. I became many things, but what I cherish the most is that I became able to see people's greatness in all things. All those mums who work every day to better the life of their family. All those migrants who leave their home country for a better life. All the Australians who do what they can to make a difference to another person's life. Every person who gives an encouraging word to someone. Today, I have the eyes to see people's greatness in all things.

## The Leap into Law

In Australia, you are not a lawyer as soon as you complete your law degree. Traditionally, you would become an articled clerk in a law firm after graduation, meaning you practice law under the supervision of an experienced lawyer for a period of time. Then, you might qualify to become a lawyer. When I completed law school, the Legal Services Board changed the entire system. In their attempt to modernize, they renamed the article clerkship to "practical legal traineeship." The traineeship included either being supervised by an experienced lawyer, participating in more study, or a mixture of both. If you successfully complete the traineeship, then you would have the privilege to ask the Supreme Court to admit you into the legal profession.

There are many things you must prove to the Supreme Court to be admitted to legal practice, including proving that you are a fit and proper person to practice law. It is not guaranteed you will be accepted. If the Supreme Court accepts your request to be admitted, you take an oath or affirmation to the Supreme Court. The last step to become an Australian Qualified Lawyer is to write your full name, sign, and date the Supreme Court's Roll, which is a huge book that contains all the names of every lawyer who has been admitted to practice. My new objective was to get my name on this Roll and become an Australian Qualified Lawyer. Easy right? Not in the slightest.

The road to becoming an Australian Qualified Lawyer had many obstacles. I did not know any law firms, I had no idea what a top-tier law firm meant, I did not have any networks in the legal industry, and I did not know the recruitment system. The law profession is a closed profession; it does not readily welcome those who do not already walk in their circles. The high school you went to mattered; the university you went to mattered; your academic record mattered. I was diving into my desired profession blind. To add to the hurdles, law firms only employed Australian citizens and permanent residents. I was neither. I was an international student. And even if I were offered a job, there wasn't a straightforward visa to apply for in order to accept the job. The Australian immigration system is geared toward skilled migration, and a guy like me straight out of university is not considered a skilled migrant. I did not know these would be my challenges when I chose to study law, but I faithfully worked through every obstacle as they arose.

## Gaining Work Experience

Toward the end of my first year of university, my friend Nick Musgrove explained to me that he would be doing work experience at a law firm called Maddocks. I had never heard of it. Nick had shared my life story with his dad, Geoff Musgrove. His dad had extended an invitation for me to join Nick to do two weeks of work experience at Maddocks. I was in shock. These were the kind of experiences all the other law students were seeking, and it was offered to me. I noticed

I was holding my breath. This shouldn't be happening to me. I am a nobody.

I had never been in a law firm before, and I had no idea what to expect. I didn't own a suit or fancy shoes. I would have to use my savings for this expense. For me, this was an opportunity of a lifetime, and I had to show up as my best.

I remember my first day at Maddocks. I arrived at 140 William St. Level 6. As I stepped off the elevator and entered the reception area, I gasped. It was like in the movies. The reception area was lavish. There were two ladies with their Britney Spears headsets. The ladies at reception offered big smiles, welcoming me in. One of the ladies at reception brought me into a meeting room. A few minutes later, Bev, a woman from HR, came down to greet me and offered me water or orange juice. I chose orange juice. How luxurious.

I was treated like I belonged. I was treated with respect. I was treated like I was the most important person in the room. It felt like a dream. There was a typed letter with my name on it, informing me that I was going to be doing work experience for two whole weeks and that I would be paid for it. This is what I'd come to Australia for: a life worth living. I finally had a taste of what my future could be like. I spent my first week in the mail room with Brett. The mail room is the heart of the law firm. So many documents printed and photocopied, letters and parcels needing to get to lawyers urgently. Everything was time sensitive. I worked hard. I never complained. I did everything asked of me. My parents had prepared me for this.

During my second week, I was with Paula in the precedents department. She is a magician. Her job was creating documents and putting code in them so that lawyers could have precedent documents and make the job of drafting letters, contracts, and emails easier, faster, and standardized. She taught me how to do this. Every document was consistent and in the same style. Everything was on brand. She was one person servicing hundreds of demanding lawyers, but nothing fazed her. Paula took me under her wing. She shared stories, told me what the lawyers were like, talked about the pitfalls of being a lawyer, and shared the culture of the firm.

Working in the mail room and precedents department was life changing for me. It was hard work. You had to keep sharp and focused all the time. Mistakes could cost millions of dollars. I learned that no matter what role we had in the organization, we each played a part to deliver exceptional legal services. Toward my last day of my work experience, I plucked up the courage to go to HR with an idea I was terrified to propose. I thanked Bev for the opportunity of work experience and went on to ask if they had any further jobs for me. I said that I would be willing to do anything. She said she would keep that in mind, and we parted ways.

## The Role That Kick-Started My Professional Journey

I got my first mobile phone when I was nineteen years old—a bright-red Nokia. I didn't want a phone. I didn't need the extra expense. It seemed to me that people used mobile phones to organize social gatherings, which I couldn't attend because I had to work. There was no point in getting a phone. In the end, I yielded. I was too lonely and was missing out on connection with my friends and missing opportunities for extra shifts at McDonald's.

Some weeks later, my phone rang. It was an unknown number. I answered it. It was Bev from Maddocks. They needed me to work. There had been an influx of work in the precedents department, and they needed someone to work with Paula. I had to check if I could make it work with my timetable as it was during the school semester, and I would be working one full day a week at Maddocks. I could make it work. I said yes.

I kept getting more and more job opportunities at Maddocks as each one finished. I worked with Sue Simmons in the debt recovery department for about two years. It was a night job from 6:00 to 9:30 p.m. We were employed by the Local Council to recover money from the local residents, whether it was fines for not voting in the election or people forgetting to pay their municipal council rates. It was a very hard job. I copped a lot of abuse from people for following up their debts. I didn't understand why people were being so mean and cruel for what they were responsible for paying. It made no sense to me. I would take a deep breath, smile, dial, and follow the script. I did my job well without supervision.

When that finished up, I worked in the library. Jeannette was head of the library at Maddocks. I was given research projects from all over the firm; I had to go to the Supreme Court at times to research obscure cases that were only kept there. I was also responsible for going to everyone's office and updating their legal loose-leaf binders. These books needed updating every time the law changed. As I made rounds through the lawyers' offices to update them, I got to learn the name of every single partner, senior associate, and lawyer. I made friends with the legal secretaries. I learned the moods of the lawyers. I learned who was friendly and open and who was closed.

During my fourth year at university, I was offered the role of paralegal, just one step removed from being a lawyer. As a law student, it didn't get any better than that. As a paralegal, I worked in a variety of different departments predominantly in both the commercial and commercial disputes departments. All this exposure allowed me to get a taste of the different sectors of law.

Over the five years I spent at Maddocks, I learned the business of law, the operations of a law firm, and how to be a lawyer.

## Competing for Success

Obtaining a summer or winter clerkship during university was an accomplishment that would distinguish you from the rest of your classmates. A clerkship was equivalent to a four-week internship in a law firm. Obtaining a clerkship is highly competitive. Statistically, only about 40 percent of law students got clerkships. Attaining a clerkship was like being part of an invite-only exclusive club. If I wanted to have a successful legal career in a top-tier law firm, I would need to get one.

There were a couple of obstacles in applying for a clerkship. The first was that I was ineligible. One of the questions asked was if I were an Australian citizen or permanent resident. I was neither. Clerkships were not available for people like me. Even if I were eligible, the other obstacle would be my grades. I had failed contracts law twice in my second year of university, both times getting 36 percent. Clerkships are offered to those who had impeccable grades: Distinctions and High Distinctions. I was sitting at a Pass. My strategy to compensate for my grades to show Maddocks that I was a hard worker was to form relationships with everyone: the partners, the senior associates, the lawyers, the legal secretaries, the mail room workers. In my view, every single person could have the potential to determine my destiny.

The clerkship system wasn't designed for people like me. I wasn't going to let the system rob me of the opportunity of being an Australian Qualified Lawyer. I set up a face-to-face meeting with Sophie Gilbert—the head of the graduate program at Maddocks. She was a beautiful, petite, blond, blue-eyed woman from New Zealand. I was twenty-one years old and incredibly nervous. When we met, I told her that I wanted to apply for a clerkship at Maddocks but was ineligible because I was not an Australian citizen or permanent resident. She found it strange that I would not be able to apply. She was on my side. She looked at me and said, "Well, I think it'd be great for the firm if you did a clerkship because of all the knowledge you have already acquired here." She said she would email me a paper form to fill out. I had overcome yet another obstacle.

Offers for clerkships happen in one specific week. All the law firms call law students offering places. It is a frenzy for both the firms as well as the students. The best law firms want the best students, and the best students want the best law firms. The firms are competing with each other, and the students are competing with each other. It was a very stressful time. The best students are offered up to six clerkships, but most students are offered none. It's hard not to take it personally if you are not offered a clerkship. As law students, we are trained to think that we are the best, the most intelligent, the leaders of tomorrow. The whole system turns us into narcists. We were willing to cheat, lie, manipulate, and destroy friendships to get this coveted opportunity in a top-tier law firm. In law school, it was hard to know who your true friends were as most people were out for themselves. The legal profession had given us our orders: get into a top-tier law firm. Failure meant that who you are is not good enough.

During this week, some of my friends were getting lots of calls with offers. I hadn't received a call. I was very anxious. My future was on the line. I couldn't go back to Zimbabwe. "There's still time," I told myself as I was walked out of the law building to go to one of my classes. Deep in thought, my bright-red Nokia rang. It was an unknown number. I thought it was probably McDonald's asking me to cover for someone who was ill. I answered. It was Sophie Gilbert.

She said, "You know why I am calling. We would like to offer you the opportunity to do a clerkship at Maddocks." I wanted to combust. I accepted her offer on the spot. I had accomplished what most international students had never accomplished: a clerkship in a top-tier Melbourne law firm. My hard work had paid off. I knew I wasn't getting this internship because of my marks because they were terrible. I knew I was getting this internship because I had worked bloody hard at Maddocks. I had been seen.

## Scrambling for Opportunities

Several months after my clerkship, I went to the United Kingdom to visit my brother. Traveling overseas was very expensive. Sharon Walker, whom I have known since I was eight years old and worked at Qantas, had put me on her travel benefits. This meant that I would get to travel if the plane was not full. Traveling on standby allowed me to travel affordably. Where flights for me could be between $2,500 or more, I could travel for around $500. This was a precious gift to me.

I intended to stay in the United Kingdom for four weeks. About a week into my holiday, I received an email from Sophie Gilbert, telling me that the firm was hosting a cocktail party for those who had participated in their clerkship program. It would be an opportunity to mingle with the partners and senior lawyers before they made their final decision to whom they would offer traineeships. There was one problem: the cocktail party was being held while I was still to be in the United Kingdom.

I knew immediately that I had to return to Australia to fight for my spot in the graduate training program. Maddocks was the only opportunity I had to work in a top-tier firm. All other doors were firmly shut. I cut my holiday short and arranged to get back to

Australia. It was mayhem. I would be traveling back to Australia on a standby ticket in peak season. The chances of me getting a flight were very slim.

Sharon helped me find a flight to Melbourne via Hong Kong, but it was not looking good as both legs of the flight were fully booked. I had to be back in Melbourne in two days. If I was successful, I would arrive the night before the cocktail party. I went to Heathrow Airport, which is one of the busiest airports in the world. I was on standby. There were about eight other people on standby, and it seemed that there would be available seats only for four. I have never prayed so hard in my life to be on a flight, and I was the third person to be called on. I had made it through the first hurdle.

Arriving in Hong Kong did not guarantee me a seat on the flight to Melbourne. I would still be on standby. When I arrived in Hong Kong, I went directly to the service counter to request a flight to Melbourne. The lady at the service counter checked her computer and told me that there was no possibility of me getting onto a flight. I was crushed. I told the lady that I needed to get onto a flight because I had an interview to attend in Melbourne for the only opportunity that would determine my future in Australia. The lady kept looking and found nothing. She looked again and said she had found something: a decommissioned seat on the flight. She investigated why it was decommissioned and found out that the tray table was broken. She offered me the seat if I were happy with a broken tray. I said I would take anything. She then said, "Oh it's also in first class." What? I would be going from Hong Kong to Melbourne in first class!

The flight was the most luxurious flight I have ever had in my life. The boy from Mutare, Zimbabwe, who only spent $500 was traveling first class. As usual, I was the only Black person in the cabin. I was also the youngest. I was treated like a king by the Qantas team. As I sat in my reclining chair sipping champagne, I prepared my strategy for the cocktail party. I replayed all the partners' names in my head and remembered what they liked to talk about. I imagined which senior associates would be there. This would be my last chance to ensure that the firm chose me. As I thought about my strategy, I fell into a deep sleep all the way home.

I flew from the United Kingdom to Melbourne to attend a party that lasted about forty-five minutes. I was nervous. I knew everyone in the room. The partners and lawyers greeted me like an old friend. The cocktail party was all chit chat about nothing in particular. They were testing us on how we connect with them. They were testing to see who they liked. I don't like chit chat. I like talking about heavy, significant things. At the cocktail party, I had to balance being witty and being lighthearted—both of which are hard for me. I don't go on the same holidays as them, I didn't go to the same schools as them, and I don't have the same culture as them. I was desperate to impress, but I had to make sure I didn't talk from desperation. I left the cocktail party feeling okay. I had done all I could to have the firm choose me. I had left no stone unturned. It was now up to the powers who be.

The process of being offered a traineeship is similar to the process of being offered a clerkship. The mood was tense at law school. It was 2008 and I was twenty-four years old. We were in the midst of the Global Financial Crisis. Some law firms were freezing hiring graduate lawyers while others were reducing the number of graduates. The environment at law school was more tense than normal. Nothing was guaranteed. One of my friends who had received several clerkships and was in the top ten of law school got no offers. We knew things were bad if he wasn't getting any offers. It all seemed random. I got a call. It was Sophie Gilbert. She offered me a position to become a graduate trainee lawyer at Maddocks. I was ecstatic. I kept this news to myself to savor the moment. By this stage in my life, I had been in Australia for nearly eight years. Eight years I had been investing my life for this one opportunity. I didn't need many opportunities—just one to take me to the next stage of creating my life in the West. Just one. I had been chosen. I was later to learn that my evaluation by the partners of the firm had brought up the most discussion. I have never found out what was discussed in the room where it happened.

I wish I could say that from here onward everything was smooth sailing, but that wasn't the case. I had accepted a job, but there was no visa for me to stay in Australia to take up the position as a graduate trainee lawyer. I realized this was probably why few international students were studying law. It was also probably why law firms at that time did not hire international students. The only visa that could have been possible at that time was called an Occupational Trainee Visa. This visa was typically used by foreigners who already had a career and wanted to meet Australian standards. Applying for this visa would be like gambling.

Six months before I completed my law degree, the universe conspired for me to stay. Prime Minister John Howard introduced what was then a radical new visa: the graduate visa. Any person who had successfully completed a university degree in Australia and had been in an Australian tertiary institution for a minimum of two years would be eligible for this special visa. The visa entitled international students to live, work, and participate in further study for eighteen months. In short, during that eighteen months, I could do whatever I wanted to do. I was

**What I did have was a vision greater than what the world told me I could have. I just kept knocking on the doors until a door opened. And I opened one door at a time.**

eligible for this visa. I was one of the first people to apply. I would be able to continue to create my life in Australia.

My dreams were coming true despite many doors being closed to me. I didn't have the money, I didn't have the visas, I didn't have the networks, I didn't have the grades, I didn't have knowledge, I didn't have the role models, I didn't even have the self-esteem—I didn't have many things. The society and environment I was living in was not designed for me to take on any of the opportunities I wanted. What I did have was a vision greater than what the world told me I could have. I just kept knocking on the doors until a door opened. And I opened one door at a time.

## Becoming an Australian Qualified Lawyer

Exactly six years after starting law school, I had my first day as a graduate trainee at Maddocks. There were ten of us who had been chosen, and I was the only Black person in the entire firm. I felt confident. Maddocks was my home. I had already spent five years of my life working there.

Our training program would be twelve months long, and it consisted of completing a Graduate Diploma in Legal Education as well as working longer than the typical thirty-eight-hour workweek. We would work in three different practice groups. I chose to work in the Commercial, Property, and Construction groups. There were four-month rotations in each practice group. Completing the training program would not guarantee an ongoing role at the firm. Our training program was like a twelve-month interview to determine if the firm liked you, as well as which partners desired you on an ongoing basis. The competition among us trainees continued. It was hard. It required perfection.

In order to succeed, trainees had to successfully complete the Graduate Diploma, be admitted as a lawyer by the Supreme Court, make money for the firm, and build good relationships with each other while pretending we were not competing.

I loved the group of trainees I was in. We supported each other. They were decent people from different walks of life. But when it came to choosing which practice groups, we would be out for ourselves. Among all the trainees, my closest friend was Vivane Karoumbalis. She was smart, hardworking, and an exceptional lawyer. We would gossip together over a cup of tea nearly every afternoon.

I successfully completed my Graduate Diploma of Legal Education. On November 17, 2009, I was admitted as an Australian Lawyer by the Supreme Court of Victoria. I was the only African in one of the most respected courtrooms in the world. I wrote my name in the Roll of the Supreme Court: Rugare Gomo. My name. My African name was added to the body of lawyers in Australia.

Like many of my accomplishments, I was alone. I had no family witness my graduation from high school. I had no family witness me graduate in my double degrees in arts and law. Once again, I had no family witness me become an Australian Qualified Lawyer. I have stood alone in my accomplishments. I don't know what it is like to have the family photo, the family party. That was not available to me. But each time, I was grateful, because I knew the world owed me nothing. I had food, a home, friends, and a community. I was safe. Whereas in Zimbabwe, there was no food or medicine, the standard of living had plummeted, and people were dying from starvation. I stood alone, and I had everything.

**I stood alone, and I had everything.**

To get an ongoing position in a practice group is like a political campaign. First, you must identify the decision makers in each department, typically the senior partner in the practice group. Then, identify who the senior partner listens to, whether it be a legal secretary or a lawyer. You must be a team player and go the extra mile. Work weekends if you must. Sacrifice your social life. Make a lot of money for the firm. Research case notes and present your findings. Be liked by clients.

Every time we changed practice groups, we were starting from scratch in building our profile and reputation. Even after we changed practice groups, it was our job to maintain and nurture the relationships we left behind. Our life was the firm. The firm was number one. We traded our lives for mingling in the right circles, the right clients, the lunches, the dinners, the fine wines. Unwittingly, we created our own bubble. We became out of touch from the world around us. We thought everything we did was important. Everything was urgent. We became enmeshed with the firm.

When the time came to find out if we would gain ongoing employment, rumor had it that the commercial group would offer three trainees ongoing positions; workplace services would offer two positions; property would offer two positions; and local government, construction, and commercial disputes would offer one position. We did the math to confirm we were all safe. We would all be getting ongoing employment at Maddocks.

I wanted to join the commercial team once I finished my traineeship. However, I felt I did not perform well. So, instead of putting the commercial group as my first preference, I picked the property group. I had been advised through my network of mentors, legal secretaries, and legal support teams not to go to the property group because it had a toxic culture. I didn't listen. I didn't like construction law. The commercial team seemed to have their eye on their favorite trainees. It seemed to me that the only opportunity would be the property group. This is one of the few times I didn't go after what I wanted. I was too scared to go for what I wanted and not be offered an ongoing opportunity.

On the day we were told which practice group had selected us, we were all nervous. We all got our first preferences, except one trainee who wasn't offered an ongoing position. We were all in shock. Now, we were nine.

It seemed that the next game was to become a partner in the firm as fast as possible. What had my life become? I seemed to have no agency about who I wanted to be or become. It seemed that the path was already created for me, and it was up to me to conform or leave. To leave would be considered weak and that you were not cut out for the profession. To leave is like telling my mum and dad I want to be a dancer and being disowned. Often, when someone left the firm, they were no longer part of the clique, the family. Never to be heard of again. It's like a death of sorts. My first year and a half as a lawyer was hell and it broke me.

Most students study law to make a difference in the world. Instead, most law students sacrifice the dream of making a difference in the world to work in a top-tier law firm that influenced every aspect of law school—to funding of social clubs, legal competitions, and awards. They tell themselves, "We will just work for a year or two, get some experience, and get out." Ten years later, with a huge mortgage, a couple of children, private school fees for the kids, and the yearly overseas trip, the vision of making a difference disappears and the daily grind is to make a lot of money to take care of the family, the social status, and the trappings of external success. On the inside, many lawyer's souls have withered away thinking that making a difference was just a childhood fantasy. So foolish to have ever thought they wanted to make a difference in the world.

## Experiences Outweigh Degrees

My journey to becoming an Australian Qualified Lawyer was greatly supported by the skills I gained in my arts degree. After failing contracts law twice, I was so scared that I was not cut out to be a lawyer. My visa didn't allow me to take a break from my studies. Instead, I created a six-month exchange program to France. I found a language school in a town called Chambery at the bottom of the French Alps, which my French lecturer approved of. My school fees in Australia for a term would cover my fees in France as well as all my living expenses. It was a win. I fully immersed myself in learning the French language, the culture, the politics, the history, and the economics. Studying all things French was my break and it would earn me credits toward my arts degree. I was inventive. The cost of my school fees for a semester in Australia would be the costs of my fees and living expenses in France. My time in France paid off in a million ways—one of them being becoming close to being fluent in French.

While I was in France, I attended a conference in Strasbourg—a symposium of the European Union's Francophonie-speaking intellectuals, ranging from politicians to members of parliament, to leaders of global not-for-profits. In those two days, I asked anyone who was running an organization if I could do an internship with them. David Fieldsend, who worked for an EU (European Union) lobby group called Care for Europe in Brussels, offered me a two-week internship. I was thrilled. Working in Brussels is still one of my favorite memories. I felt like I was part of something big. The EU represents an institution that is doing its best to promote peace, freedom, equality, security, and opportunity for its citizens irrespective of its past, its wars with each other, and its cultural and linguistic differences. I dreamed that maybe Africa would be like the EU one day. Maybe us Africans can live in peace and prosperity one day. I pondered what kind of leader I could be.

Being away from law school was healing for me. I was less stressed, and my grades improved considerably. When I returned to Australia, I decided to do an honors thesis in law on the rise of ethnicism on the African continent, a dissertation on the EU's "illegal immigration policy," and a joint honors thesis called "la Constitution Européenne est morte" (the European Constitution is dead). This added an extra year to my university degree and extra costs, but immersing myself in these research opportunities sharpened my mind and helped me form ideas about the kind of person I want to be in the world.

**No one can take away who I became.**

My degrees are valuable, but the experiences I went through to obtain my degrees and the journey to becoming an Australian Qualified Lawyer are priceless. No one can take away who I became. It was a journey filled with good things, bad things, and the art of turning bad things into good things. Looking back, the hardest thing I faced during this period of my life wasn't my degree; it wasn't raising money; it wasn't getting into a law firm. The hardest thing I faced was confronting that I am a gay man.

# CHAPTER 5

## Striving for Authenticity

To be gay is worse than being a rapist. To be gay is the ultimate sin. To be gay is synonymous with pedophile. To be gay is to live in fear that people will beat me up and kill me. To be gay is to bring the highest form of shame upon my family and community. To be gay is to be an outcast. To be gay is to have zero opportunities. To be gay is an idea to be eradicated. This is what many people have said about being gay. These are the things I once believed of myself.

I am crowned with many names for being gay: faggot, girly boy, poofter, cocksucker, homo, fairy, sodomite.

Before 2001, no country in the world permitted same-sex marriage. In Zimbabwe, if men had any sexual relations with each other, it is punishable by physical beatings and imprisonment. In some countries today, being gay is punishable by death. The message I received from the world, at home, at church, at school, with friends, on TV, in Zimbabwe, in Australia, and in every fabric of society is that to be gay is an abomination. What do we do with abominations? We eradicate them.

I have lived my entire life in fear of being eradicated.

## The Evolution of My Sexuality

As I was going through puberty, my dreams were of men. I thought these dreams where just a phase and that they would disappear when I was grown. I never spoke of them with anyone. I completely suppressed and ignored what was happening to me. No one had prepared me for puberty. I didn't know that I would have wet dreams. I didn't know there would be changes to my body. I didn't know that I would develop a sexuality. My wet dreams were my secret. I loved them, but I was ashamed of them. All I knew was to be silent because if someone deemed that these kinds of dreams were inappropriate, I feared I would be eradicated.

I discovered masturbation at nineteen years of age. I loved it, but I was ashamed. Masturbation for me was the same as having sex before marriage, which was seen as taboo and shameful. Shame on the person and on the family for raising a person who could not control their sexual urges. Masturbation conflicted with my values. Even though nobody knew I was masturbating, God knew. I was sure there was no redemption.

I mostly lived my life pretending I was not a sexual being and denied any thoughts I had about men. This all came to a head when I went to France for my exchange program in my third year of university. In France, I had to confront the one thing I never ever wanted: I am a gay man.

\* \* \*

When I was twenty, I lived in France for six months in a small town called Chambery. It was wintertime, and it was freezing. I was on one of my weekend adventures. I decided to visit a town called Grenoble about forty-five minutes away. While I was standing by the heaters warming my hands waiting for the train to arrive to take me to Grenoble, a guy next to me wearing a rainbow scarf started chatting with me. I was thrilled. I always relished the opportunity to practice my French. Coincidentally, our train tickets had us sitting opposite each other on the train ride, so we continued our conversation. Before we went our separate ways in Grenoble, we exchanged email addresses and phone numbers so that we could keep in touch with one another.

When I arrived home that night, there was an email already waiting for me in my inbox from my new friend. I was excited. In his email, he said in French, "You are the most beautiful person I've ever met. I live 20 minutes away. It'd be wonderful for us to connect and get to know you and be intimate with you." I was horrified. I was disgusted. I felt dirty inside. I didn't know what to do. I couldn't imagine what I did or what I said for this guy to think I would want to have sexual relations with him. I collapsed in my chair staring at my computer in shock. What was it about me that had him send that email? Why did he think I was gay? After I took a few moments to recover, I typed an email back. I said, "Thank you very much for your email. I am not a gay. I'm a Christian and it's wrong to be gay. Thank you." I got an email back where this person was very abusive toward me. It is said that we hate what we hate about ourselves.

\* \* \*

Linda was a friend of mine from Germany. We were studying French together. She invited me for lunch one day and she made this beautiful

German goulash. She sat me down, placed the food in front of me, and said bluntly, "Everybody in the institute wants to know if you are gay." I was scared. I had to think quickly on my feet to protect myself. I looked at her and I responded, "No, I am not gay." She looked at me. She smiled and nodded, and we continued our lunch. I didn't enjoy the rest of my goulash. I was rattled. What was happening to me? Why does it seem that everyone has this sudden interest in my sexuality, and worse they think I am gay.

\* \* \*

In 2005, in Australia, you had to go to a video store to rent DVDs to watch the latest movies. These were the times before online streaming services like Netflix. In France, you could rent a DVD like taking money from an ATM machine. It was private. Nobody could see what videos you were browsing. As I was browsing French videos, I stumbled across the X-rated DVDs. I was curious. I told myself not to browse that section, but my curiosity got the better of me. What I was doing was wrong. I was being lustful. Lust is a sin. I came across gay pornography. I felt a rush in my head. I debated with myself if I should borrow the DVD or not. No one was watching me. I was in a foreign country. No one knew me. I rented it. It was my secret. When I got to my apartment, I watched the DVD when my housemate was gone. I was shocked, excited, and ashamed of what I saw. I had never felt this kind of rush in my head before. I was hooked. My evil was escalating. I returned the DVD as soon as possible, but I thought about the images continually. This began my cycle of borrowing gay porn DVDs, enjoying them, being filled with feelings of shame, and feeling disconnection with myself and God, returning them, obsessively thinking about them, and compulsively borrowing them again.

I never admitted to myself that I was a gay. I was just happening to watch gay DVDs. I told myself that all of this would stop when I got married to a woman. I was sure of it.

* * *

I was visiting Nice in the South of France. I was taking photos of everything using my digital Fujifilm camera. A man approached me and said to me in French, "I can help take photos of you so that you can have some pictures of yourself in Nice." "What a good idea," I thought. I thanked him profusely. Afterward, he asked whether I wanted to have a coffee with him. I agreed, seeing it yet as another opportunity to practice my French with a French person. Off we went to a café. He took me to McDonald's. This was odd for me. With all the plethora of cafes in France going to McDonald's was so *un-French*. I said nothing.

When we sat down at *McDo* as the French call it, I had expected him to sit opposite me, but much to my surprise, he sat right beside me. Suddenly, he grabbed my hand publicly and looked at me as he told me how soft my hands were. His knee started rubbing against my leg. I was horrified. I froze. I didn't know what to say or do. If I stood up and left, I felt that would be impolite. A good Christian boy does not embarrass their elders. I was stuck. I looked at the waiter in front of me, silently pleading with him to save me. But of course, nothing happened. It was all in my head. He then stood up, went into the McDonald's bathroom, and propositioned for me to come in.

By this time, I knew something was really wrong. I refused to enter the bathroom, but I stood outside frozen. My brain refused to think. I still didn't know what to do. I just stood there stunned. I came up with a plan. When he came out of the bathroom, he asked what I was doing next. I lied to him. I told him that I needed to go because I had my next engagement. I was terrified that he was going to find out I was lying. I felt so vulnerable. I didn't know if he was going to follow me.

Once I finally escaped his presence, I aimlessly walked around the streets in Nice. I found a double-decker bus, I got in, went to the top, and sat down. I was so ashamed. What had I done to attract this man's attention? What was it about me that he thought he could proposition me? Why were men seeking my attention? I figured I was being punished by God for masturbating and watching pornography. I blamed myself for everything that just happened.

Deep in shame and deep in thought, I concluded that what was happening to me was not my fault. It was God's fault. The Bible says that we are all made perfectly in God's image. My logical conclusion was that I wasn't made perfectly in God's image. If I had been made perfectly in God's image, I wouldn't masturbate, I wouldn't watch gay porn, I wouldn't be having feelings toward men. I was a degenerate. If I am a degenerate, I no longer needed to follow God's rules—I was going to hell anyway where degenerates belong. I decided to free myself of the constraints of Christianity and explore my sexuality as soon as I got back home to Melbourne.

\* \* \*

To question my sexuality is the bravest thing I have ever done in my life. I wanted to remain blind to who I am. It is easier to follow the well-trodden path. It comes with many benefits: love from family, approval from friends, career opportunities, climbing up the social ladder. But this well-trodden path couldn't give me one thing: happiness. I had reached a crossroad. The guilt and shame were killing me. Simply put, confront who I am or kill myself. I could no longer ignore that there was something different about me. I never wanted to be gay. To be gay meant that I would have to question every single value I had blindly followed. I didn't have the strength for that. I chose life with the tiniest littlest flame that was still inside of me. It was overwhelming. If I were gay, what other beliefs would I question? What would I think about abortion? What would I think about the death penalty? What if God didn't exist? What would I think about gay conversion camps? What were my views about working for money? To question my sexuality was my first step to questioning all my core beliefs. I was having an existential crisis.

## Confronting My Sexuality

I decided to explore my sexuality when I was back in Australia. I didn't know anybody who was gay. I was a Christian; Uncle Andrew was a Christian. I thought that if Uncle Andrew ever found out I was gay, I would be kicked out of home and perhaps have to go back to Zimbabwe to nothing. I was terrified.

I didn't know how to meet other gay people, so I searched online. I found a gay chat room. I was so scared of being found out that I created a fake persona. I invented this personality that I was a South African British, had a fake name, and used a different accent. I had one rule: meet a person once and never meet again.

My first hookup with a guy was awful. We met in the chatroom. He picked me up close to my home. The moment I met him, I was disgusted. He smoked. He was extremely thin like a drug user, and he was disheveled. I felt powerless to turn back. I felt obliged to continue because I had to keep my agreements and I can't have someone older than me feel disrespected. We had oral sex at his home. I couldn't wait to just get home, take a shower, and go to bed. I was profoundly disgusted. I could smell him on me for over a week—a painful reminder of what an evil person I am. I promised myself never to do it again. Two weeks later, I was back on the chat looking for my next hookup. I would be filled with shame every single time and I would swear I would never do it again. I continued the cycle for the next six months.

Two of the most powerful false twin gods are shame and hopelessness. They exist to destroy all things in their entirety. They hold no prisoners. The one objective of shame and hopelessness is suicide. The most cunning part about shame and hopelessness is their ability to convince us people to kill ourselves and each other without even knowing it. We are so used to the traditional forms of suicide: taking pills, jumping off a bridge. But that is not the only form of suicide. Overdrinking, over smoking, overeating are all forms of suicide. Any unhealthy thing we do to escape from our reality is a kind of death. "At least I did not jump of the bridge," I would say to feel better about myself. However, every time I had sex, I was killing myself, my spirit, my mental health, my emotional well-being, my physical health. My life was hopeless. My life in Australia felt worse than had I stayed in Zimbabwe.

My sexual encounters were always done in secret, and they were dangerous. I would leave the house at night without telling anybody. If something ever happened to me, nobody would be able to find out where I was. I'd meet men in car parks, in public parks, in public toilets. My actions were dangerous, all because I just wanted to be able to express my sexuality. Sometimes, the only places available were in public places, which could have been raided by the police at any time. My sexual experiences and my relationship to sex became one of high risk. Sex is meant to be an enjoyable experience. In the moment, it was enjoyable. But the aftermath of it was always horrible because I was crippled with paralyzing shame. Little did I know that this would be the beginning of the manifestation of my addiction to sex.

I wish I could have been like my other friends, my straight friends who seemed to have stable relationships and proudly talked about their sex lives with no shame. That was not me. My experience of sex was always in the shadows. Exploring my sexuality really altered the way I saw the world. Growing up in Zimbabwe, lying is a bad thing to do. Deception is a bad thing. And here I was, now twenty-one years old, exploring my sexuality and lying about who I was. I was deceiving people as well as manipulating them for my sexual gratification. But the men I was meeting up with were deceiving others as well. Many of the men I met up with, some of them had girlfriends, and some of them were married. But they too did not feel safe, and they didn't have the courage to come out as gay men.

During my first six months of being sexually active, I had easily met with over fifty men. That meant hours of going onto a computer, going into a chat room, finding a man to meet, arranging a location, going there, having a sexual liaison with them, coming back home, and then doing it again. My life became unmanageable. My mental health suffered, my grades suffered, my work suffered, and my relationships suffered.

In the early nineties, one in four adults in Zimbabwe were HIV positive. And here I was in Australia, having sexual relations with multiple men. All I could think of was, "Am I putting myself at risk for getting infected with HIV and STIs?" I thought I was going to become HIV positive and die of AIDS. I didn't want that for myself, but I couldn't seem to stop.

\* \* \*

At the end of my third year of university, I became very sick. I woke up one day with a shooting pain in my left leg. It started swelling. As the day progressed, the pain moved throughout my body. I couldn't move. When I tried to move my arm, it felt like my limbs were breaking. When I was touched, it felt as if electricity was being pumped through my body. I was in excruciating pain, and I started screaming. I went to the hospital and met with some doctors who asked me a lot of questions. One of the questions they asked me was regarding my sexual activity. And even more precisely was whether I was having sex with men. In that moment, I had a choice: to lie or to tell the truth.

I knew that I had to give the facts so that they could do the proper tests they needed to do. I told the truth. I whispered, "I have sex with men." I was so ashamed. This was the first time I was being forced to admit publicly what I was doing. And this would be put on my medical record. Worse was that the doctors conducted several tests but they couldn't find anything wrong with me. So, a different set of doctors came, and then they asked the same questions. "Are you having sex with men?" "Yes, I'm having sex with men," I repeated. This happened about eight times in the one period. I was ashamed and frightened. I was being forced to repeat this answer over and over and over again. At one stage, I even yelled at the doctor, "Don't talk to me. Talk to the other doctors. I've already told them what's wrong with me." Every time the doctors asked me the question, it was traumatic. I was sure I was going to be eradicated.

My first night in the hospital, they put me on a morphine drip, but I could still feel the pain. Three days later, I got discharged from the hospital. The doctors had no idea what was wrong with me. All the blood tests came back negative. All my STI tests came back negative. So, they had no idea what was happening. What they could see was that my white blood cell count was high, and it looked like my body was initially fighting an infection but now my white blood cells were attacking my body. Nobody could figure it out. I got discharged from the hospital and I went back home. For the next three months, I was bedridden, because I still couldn't move my body. I had to be carried to the toilet every time I had to go to the bathroom. I had to be washed in the shower because I couldn't move my limbs without excruciating pain.

I was on a regimen of Panadeine Forte every four hours because the pain was unbearable. I ended up going to Monash Hospital as part of their outpatient program, where there was a whole group of doctors working on me. I had infectious disease working on me, I had dermatology working on me, and I had rheumatology working on me. All the tests you can imagine that could be possibly done to me were being carried out. I was their lab rat, and I was in pain. My mystery illness completely altered my life. I thought that God was now finally punishing me for all my sexual activity, all my lies, my deception, my manipulation of men for my sexual gratification. I felt completely and utterly alone.

## Death and Rebirth

I spent the next three months visiting doctors. Each visit was the same. Every week I'd get examined, have my blood drawn, and be told the following week that they didn't know what was wrong with me. When the rheumatologist wanted to put me on steroids, I was initially excited. I had this fantasy in my head that I was going to take the pills and put muscle mass on my skinny frame. Unfortunately, when I Googled the side effects of prescription steroids, I learned that the opposite was true. I could gain an unhealthy amount of weight, my bones could be thinned, I'd be susceptible to diseases, and potentially have a hump on the back of my neck. That is when I hit rock bottom. I remember the moment when I decided I was no longer going to participate in these medical experiments. I felt so defeated and helpless.

I remember having this one-sided conversation with myself saying that if I'm being punished by God, then I no longer deserve the opportunity to be free. I no longer deserve the opportunity to remain in Australia. I no longer deserve the opportunity to create a wonderful life for myself here. I was not worthy. I had failed. I'd been given this opportunity and I felt I had abused it because of my relationships with other men. The entire time I was sick, I never accepted that I was gay. When people asked me if I was gay, I denied it. When the doctors asked me, I'd tell them that I was having sex with other men, but this did not mean I was gay. I always thought that when I found the right woman, all these uncomfortable feelings would disappear. That never happened. I surrendered to my death. When I surrendered was when I finally accepted that I was a gay man.

Once I accepted that I was gay, I miraculously started getting better. I learned to walk again. What would take me an hour to walk fifty meters now took only twenty minutes. I was able to eventually jog and run. Since then, I haven't gone a day without being grateful for my ability to move. To me, it's a demonstration of my surrender to being a gay man.

\* \* \*

My friend Jess came to visit me at home when I was still recovering from my illness. In my early days of university, I thought she would be a perfect person to marry. Jess is intelligent, asks the most interesting questions, seemed liberated and free to use her voice, and is pleasing to my eyes. My ideal wife. I was on a stretcher bed in the garden when she came to visit. She brought a chair to sit alongside me to keep me company. At this time, we were not very close friends, but we were part of the same friendship group. We started talking and then there was a brief moment of silence.

She looked at me and said, "Can I please tell you something that I haven't told many people?" I looked up at her and I said, "Of course, anything." She said, "I am a lesbian." Her announcement was shocking to me. How could this beautiful, intelligent woman be a lesbian? I never expected that. I looked at her and whispered, "I'm gay." From that day onward, we became the closest of friends. She became my best friend. In the gay community, many people at that time were committing suicide, taking drugs, and overdrinking.

Jess and I made a pact early on in our friendship. Three simple things: do not kill ourselves because of our sexual identity, do not take drugs to escape our pain, and be the best gay role models we could be for those who come after us. These three promises have been a guiding light for us over the past twenty years.

Eventually, Jess and I decided that it was time for us to reveal our true selves. How could we be role models for other gay people if we ourselves were still hiding? We were bloody scared, but we knew if anything went sideways, we always had each other. For me, coming out meant coming out to my university friends, Uncle Andrew, all my Christian friends, my brother in the United Kingdom, and my family who were living in South Africa. All I knew was that I thought most people believed that being gay is an abomination and abominations need to be eradicated.

I jumped. I jumped for freedom.

## Coming Out

I could no longer pretend that I was not a gay man. I talked to every single person that was important to me personally because I wanted to be in control of my own story. I'll never forget the fear I felt before I came out to my friends and my family.

I came out to over twenty of my friends and, in turn, I received a variety of responses. Some of them were like, "Duh, we've always known you were gay. We were just waiting for you to come out to us." That was a huge relief.

Coming out to my brother was messy. It did not go the way I wanted it to go. In fact, my brother caught me with another man in his home. I was terrified and ashamed because now I couldn't control the situation. I had been so scared of telling my brother that I was gay and so I was using sex to numb my fear. Sex was my drug of choice to escape pain. All the conversations I had practiced with myself leading up to coming out to my brother disappeared. I simply said, "By the way, I'm gay." He said he already knew.

When I came out to my mum, she had no idea I was gay. I was compelled to explain to her that there was nothing wrong with me—that I did not have a mental illness. My mom said, "You have to understand, Rugare, I don't hate that you're gay and I don't love that you're gay. I know nothing about it." Just like me, my mom had no awareness of what it was like to be homosexual. My dad reacted unexpectedly when I came out to him. He said, "You're still my son. I love you. You're still my son." My sister was around thirteen years old when I came out to her. She was not surprised. She reminded that on one of my rare visits, she had asked me why I walked like Tyra Banks.

Coming out is one of the bravest things I have done in my life. Coming out was revealing a part of myself that many people in society said should be eradicated. I am not the only brave person.

The woman who chooses not to have children when society tells her to have children is brave. The person who chooses to marry outside their culture is brave. The men who share their emotions in a culture where men are only allowed to show bravado are brave. Choosing not to take drugs and be blind drunk every weekend in a culture that glorifies alcohol is brave. How will you be brave today?

## Freedom

What did revealing my true self make available for my life? Where there had been disconnection, I felt connection. Where there had been fear, there was peace. Where there was mistrust, there was trust. Where there was dishonesty, there was openness and transparency. I was adulting. I was claiming who I was irrespective of what that world told me I could not be or what I thought the world told me I could not be. It is in these moments of courage and authenticity I got to find the pure love of people. Most people are good people. Despite people like me all around the world still living in utter fear of being eradicated, in Northern Nigeria, Uganda, Qatar, and Russia. In this lifetime, despite the predominant conversation that I should be eradicated, I learned that love is to be found everywhere, with Muslims, Jews, Christians, Hindus, Zimbabweans, Australians, straight people, Black people, white people, all people. Taking the risk to discover who I am and discover that I am a gay man opened me up to what most people in the world are searching for and which I have found: love. Nobody can take that away from me. It's mine because I dared to be me.

I am always grateful for the women's rights movement. Without women rights, there are no gay rights. Women's rights opened the door for me to be free. I believe that my freedom must elevate the freedom of others. My freedom must elevate the freedom of our First Nations people. My freedom must elevate the freedom of trans-people. My freedom must elevate the freedom of Albino people who are murdered for spiritual rituals. My freedom must elevate the freedom of neurodiverse people. My freedom must elevate the lives of people with disabilities. My freedom must elevate girls' lives in Africa and the Middle East. My freedom opens the doors for all people to be free.

**I stand firm for free. I will always be me.**

I stand firm for free. I will always be me.

# CHAPTER 6

# Creating Opportunity by Leaving the Law

## My Time as a Property Lawyer

The property group at Maddocks had a bad reputation in the firm, but I thought I could handle it. The biggest downfall of this group was that it was cliquey. It was like going to high school and having an in-group and an out-group. If you were part of the in-group, you'd be taken out to lunch with the partners, you'd get high-quality work given to you, and you were praised and celebrated for your achievements. If you were part of the out-group, you were not going out for lunch with the partners. You'd work very, very hard with very little praise, and mostly everything that you did wrong was pointed out to you regularly. I was part of the out-group.

My whole life I'd been a hard worker, and whenever there was an opportunity for me to seize, I zeroed in on it and did what I had to do to attain it. I took the actions to get those opportunities and for those opportunities to materialize. However, in the property group, no matter how hard I worked, the opportunities were not coming my way. There were no opportunities to meet with the clients and that precious one-on-one time with the senior partners was nonexistent. In the property group, I had no community. I was alone. Going into work was dreadful because I knew at some point in the day, somebody was going to point out how bad I was at my job. Each day, my self-worth was being chipped away one piece at a time.

I pretended that I had it all together. After all, we had invested so much time and money for me to have this opportunity to become an Australian Qualified Lawyer. It had been nine years since I'd left my family and I'd overcome so many obstacles. With the help of others, I'd invested over $120,000 in my education, and I was so afraid of disappointing those who helped me arrive here. I felt I couldn't leave.

Many, many lawyers in the same program were going through exactly what I was going through. We had different ways of coping. Some numbed their pain by using drugs and alcohol, and I was using sex to numb my feelings. Sex served as a coping mechanism for me, and while I knew it was unhealthy, I continued to abuse sex to make myself feel better about my situation. To make matters worse, I now had money to facilitate my habits and I would spend countless hours scanning men on apps. At times, I would fly to Sydney for a single hookup, and I would even insert myself in other gay people's relationships.

I was spending a lot of time involved in sexual encounters that never led to connection or love, and that made me feel worse about myself. I desperately wanted connection, even if I didn't know it at the time. The fact that I was engaging with others on a strictly physical level with no potential for a future made me feel even more alone and this was exasperated at the property group, as nobody there was interested in connecting on a friendship level. Lawyers at the firm simply walked around in their posh power suits, groomed to the nines, with so little vulnerability that they appeared robotic, unavailable for any type of real connectivity outside of the office. And like all things that weren't serving me over time, I let go of this job with no regrets.

## Courage to Leave Maddocks

I remember clearly when I made the decision to leave the law. I was sitting in a construction dispute meeting. After I had been working so hard on researching how to resolve the dispute, none of the disputing parties were interested in the advice of either lawyer. Both parties failed to take the advice, and instead of listening, they were set on spewing hate toward one another. They despised each other so much that they ended up taking the matter to court. That is the moment I realized I was wasting my life as a lawyer. The opposing lawyer and our team had spent so many hours creating a plan that would make a difference to our respective clients, but our clients were more interested in their egos and ignored our advice. In this environment, I would not be seen or heard. I decided that day that to have power, I need to be a decision maker. This decision changed my life forever, but I didn't know it then.

A mentor of mine within the property group encouraged me to leave. He would always say, "Rugare, do not stay in the law firm for too long. There are beasts. Don't be like me. I'm trapped. I kept on getting paid more money. Now I've got a mortgage and I've got all these responsibilities, and I don't feel I can leave. Don't do that. Get the training and leave." I would listen, take it in, but not really take him seriously. It wasn't until I had been with the property group for two years when I actually realized what he was referring to. I, too, was starting to feel trapped.

Another turning point for me came when it was time to meet about my performance review. Because of the global financial crisis, there had been a pay freeze in the firm for about two years and the partners in the property group had decided not to give me a pay rise in line with the other people at my year level. While the rest of the associates in my year level were going to be getting $80,000, I was only going to be getting $70,000, and they justified this because my performance was bad.

Yes, my performance was bad. I didn't want to admit to myself that my performance had been atrocious. If I admitted that my performance was bad, I felt helpless to do anything about it. I didn't have the support I needed. I could barely wake up in the morning to go to work. I was late regularly. My drafting of contracts and leases had mistakes. I would have long coffee breaks and that meant I was not meeting my billing target regularly. I always shamed myself for my performance for not being enough. After my performance review, I realized that my lack of performance wasn't wholly my fault. I was in a toxic environment. I don't blame the property group; I was opportunistic by choosing this group and it had come to bite me hard in the butt. This was an impetus for me to find my way out and find a firm with a great environment that would allow me to thrive. I knew I could thrive. After everything I had accomplished and after all the obstacles I had overcome, coming to Australia, getting a visa, completing my law degree, becoming an Australian Qualified Lawyer, I knew I could do it.

Another thing that spurred me to leave was my volunteer role with the Asylum Seeker Resource Centre (ASRC). I had been volunteering with the ASRC as a volunteer solicitor for about two years. I was helping applicants from the African continent and the French-speaking communities like the Democratic Republic of Congo,

Nigeria, and Zimbabwe apply for asylum. I loved my job, but it was heartbreaking. Every week, I would hear their brave stories. Nothing I have ever accomplished compares to what they have had to do to be free. The Nigerian who had fled the country because he was going to be killed for the practice of his faith. I heard of people from my own home country who had fled because they had witnessed their family being killed. The stories were life and death stories. Using my best mind and skills for them to get asylum was critical. There was no room for error. If they did not get the asylum and share their story with me so that they could get the asylum, they could be in detention indefinitely, and that was going to be on me. So, I worked bloody hard on all those asylum cases as a volunteer solicitor. As I was working on their applications, I became aware of my own circumstances at work. I was tolerating being in a prison; they were not. I summoned the courage to take a new action to free myself, just like they had taken actions to free themselves.

* * *

I remember when I was in the office, my phone rang. I picked it up and a lady introduced herself as someone from the Department of Immigration. Immediately I thought, "Oh no, what have I done wrong?" She explained to me that they were ready to process my permanent residency because lawyers had been put back on the skills in demand list. This meant that they were going to fast track my application. I had been waiting two years for my application to be processed. I had to do a health test and a criminal check again, and once those had come back successfully, my permanent residency would be granted.

On August 16, 2011, my permanent residency was granted. I felt free. I was now twenty-six years old. It had taken over ten years to become an Australian permanent resident. Ten years terrified of having to go back to Zimbabwe to nothing. I had made it. I had made it in the West. I could remain in Australia indefinitely. I could apply for any job I wanted. I could go to university and the government would pay for it. I had access to healthcare. I could buy a house. I could access welfare. I could move to New Zealand permanently if I wanted to. I could change careers. I could love whomever I wanted. I was free to become whoever I wanted to be. August 16, 2011, is when I was born free.

## Harwood Andrews

In September 2011, I started a new job in another law firm called Harwood Andrews. Harwood Andrews was an improvement to the quality of my life, but there was still something missing. Over time, I learned that traditional law firms are the same. In a law firm, you have people at the top dictating every aspect of the organization, and it results in a loss of individuality within the firm. If you don't conform to this type of culture, you'd be fired. I always wondered why many lawyers would bounce around to different law firms. I now know what they have been seeking is a sense of individuality, independence, and dare I say freedom. In these traditional firms, all the rules and ideas come from the top and are imposed on the rest of the law firm—no different from a dictatorship. I soon quickly realized that I could never be free working in a law firm.

At the time, I thought I should just suck it up and be happy. I was an Australian Qualified Lawyer and had my Australian permanent residency, but the longer I continued to work in the law, the more I felt this profound sense of unfulfillment. I started questioning my entire purpose. Is this what my life was going to be like forever? I have done everything right, but why do I feel so unhappy? I have followed my dreams so why do I feel stuck?

It was painful. I was profoundly unhappy and unfulfilled and deep down I knew that I needed to interrupt my journey. Sometimes in life, you have no idea that you're unfulfilled, or that you're purposeless. You just have this sense that there's something missing, but you can't articulate it. And oftentimes when we question our fulfillment, we sink into a sea of feeling like we are ungrateful, and from there, a whirlwind of guilt sets in. There I was, in a career I only dreamed about in a country with far more opportunity than I ever imagined, and yet, I was still unfulfilled. So many people had helped me get to this point, and if anything, I should keep going to show them I'm thankful for all they sacrificed for me. I had food on my table, I had a place to live, I was at a reputable law firm, and I was generating more money than ever before. Yet, there I was feeling unhappy.

Up until this point, my entire life revolved around becoming a successful lawyer. And now I was. But inside I felt alone, trapped, scared, and dead. While I was at Harwood Andrews, the Property Institute of Victoria introduced a new program, the first of its kind. It was a mentoring program for young people in the property industry. I applied, and out of eight hundred applicants, I was one of twenty-five who was selected. Along with the twenty-five other people from the property industry, I was going to be matched up with a leader in the property industry. The goal of the program was to develop young guns to become titans in the property industry. When I applied for this program, I was feeling a sense of purposelessness, and I thought this program would light some fire under me and drive me to move ahead in my career with motivation.

Soon after I was selected, a behavior consultant matched me up to my new mentor. That is when I met Roz Hansen, who was an international urban planner. Roz's first impression on me was unforgettable. When I first walked into the room to meet her, she was wearing a leopard-print outfit. She had orange-reddish hair. Her presence consumed every inch of the room. I was thrilled. Finally, someone who was free. We were a match made in heaven. Roz saw me for who I was. In our first conversation, she looked at me and said, "There's nothing that you have said to me that has told me that you're passionate about a property career, but I can hear that you love making a difference in other people's lives." I looked at her and I didn't know whether to affirm it or not. Was it wrong that I was in a mentoring program that was designed to take my career to the next level in the property industry, and wasn't quite sure I was really meant to be there? I was afraid of getting kicked out of the mentoring program but had the courage to say, "Yes, I really want to make a difference to other people, and I don't think I've found my calling yet."

She smiled and said, "I know I'm meant to take your career in property to the next level. We're not going to do that. We're going to go on a different adventure to explore what's possible for you." My heart leapt with joy when I heard those words. I felt for the first time like somebody was hearing me and seeing me for exactly who I was. I no longer had to follow the legal template of success. I could now follow my heart's template of success. One thing I realized when working with Roz was that even though I had now accomplished what I had wanted to accomplish since I was a fourteen-year-old boy coming to Australia, I still didn't know what to do with the rest of my life. I lacked direction, but found it again when I met Roz Hansen, who became my biggest champion. She inspired hope that I could leave the legal profession and move into the business community or pursue whatever I wanted. My mentorship with Roz changed the entire course of my life.

## Creating a New Life

I didn't know what I wanted to be or do. On the journey, I thought that I may want to be a property developer. When we started exploring this avenue, I started having panic attacks. I started having feelings of depression like I had when I worked in the property group at Maddocks. This avenue wasn't for me. We firmly closed that door.

It took me nearly a year to articulate what I wanted to be and do. It seemed to come down to two things: I wanted to be a decision maker and I wanted to help people. The how is what escaped me. This is where having amazing mentors is important, because you can't think what you don't know. Roz introduced me to her expansive network. She seemed to know everyone. She knew the Premier of Victoria, members of parliament from all parties, business leaders, and billionaire families. People either loved her or feared her. There was no in between. Roz reminded me of my grandmother—loving, hardworking, and couldn't tolerate idiots. Roz had accomplished what my grandmother was never allowed to be: a leader. Roz led men, she led women, and she led all people. Roz was like me—she had been the only woman in the room, the only woman on the board, and the lone voice in a male-dominated industry. She used her power; she used it well. She used it to uplift people and destroy the status quo. Roz had earned the industry's respect because she had worked bloody hard.

I networked like crazy for nearly a year, learning a million lessons and meeting some of the finest people in life. But no concrete opportunities came out of it. The feedback I kept on getting was that "I was a wild card." What does that even mean? The business community kept saying that they could see I was talented but were hesitant to give me a chance because I didn't tick their recruiting processes. For example, I didn't have an MBA, or I had no work experience in the industry. This is when I really discovered how conservative corporate Australia was.

Corporate Australia failed to appreciate the power of my life experience and the soft and hard skills I had acquired, which were more valuable than an MBA. They failed to see that I was a person who could turn mud into gold. They failed to see that I was more valuable than five people on the same job. Corporate Australia keeps itself small and disconnected from the world by the boxes they tick, boxes that don't reflect Australia's rich, multicultural society, wealth of knowledge, and experience. Corporate Australia underestimated me. I felt I was back in my headmaster's office in Zimbabwe when he told me that if I went to Australia there was a chance I would kill myself.

In the spaces where I thought I should be seen, most people have underestimated me. I now know it has nothing to do with me. When I stop seeking people's validation and approval, I have now come to see these reactions as people's own fears, biases and lack of exposure, knowledge, and wisdom. These people, these businesses are following the well-trodden path irrespective of if that path leads off a cliff. At twenty-seven years old without this wisdom, I felt defeated. Something needed to change. I was still clinging to my legal career with one hand and not fully letting go. This was not fair for Harwood Andrews nor for me. I drew the line in the sand. I gave my resignation notice at Harwood Andrews. I had two months of savings, and I created a game for myself that I was going to find a job within two months, no matter what, no back door. This was going to be the making of me. I was either going to succeed or fail. I was scared.

One month went by and no opportunities came. When I was down to my last two weeks before I ran out of money, an opportunity presented itself in the oddest of ways. In addition to being a volunteer solicitor with the Asylum Seeker Resource Centre, I was on the board of the Australian-African Business Council of Victoria. Its mission was to facilitate and promote trade between Australia and African countries. We regularly met Australian and African ambassadors and held events on opportunities for business for Australian countries in Africa or for African countries in Australia. I loved being part of the Australian-African Business Council. It made me feel like I was a diplomat.

After I quit my job, the President of the Australian-African Business Council (Vic), Di, had recently accepted a role as the Executive Director of a Foundation. The Foundation was building peace centers in different African countries. They also had a children's literacy program where African children would write the stories of their own ancestors. Di asked me if I was open to volunteering to help with the Foundation. How could I say no? I love books. However, I never grew up reading many African stories. The one book I read in Zimbabwe was by a Nigerian author, Chinua Achebe, titled *Things Fall Apart*. I imagined what it would be like for an African child to write their own stories and have them published rather than reading the stories from solely Europe. The fact that there was going to be an inter-African continental exchange of these stories was incredibly exciting for me. I offered to volunteer one day a week while I was looking for my job.

The Foundation also had a commercial arm, which was creating leadership, business, and management courses by interviewing global leaders around the world and filming case studies. It included people like Noble Prize Winner Archbishop Desmond Tutu, former Prime Minister of Australia John Howard, World Famous Illusionist David Copperfield, and Under-Secretary to the United Nations Baroness Amos to name a few. This would allow students everywhere to have access to the voices of global leaders. It was like democratizing knowledge. What a vision, I thought.

On one of the days I was volunteering with the Foundation, I had an opportunity to give a presentation in my capacity as a board member of the Australian-African Business Council for the new Australian High Commissioner to Nigeria. I put my heart and my soul into this brief to circulate to all the attendees. I researched things about trade and highlighted opportunities between Nigeria and Australia. On the day of the meeting, I was in the room with the Australian High Commissioner to Nigeria, Di, the President of the Australian-African Business Council, and the man who was both the Founder of the Foundation and the education business. The meeting was off the charts. Everybody was impressed with what I had created.

After the presentation, Di, the founder, and I were walking back to the office on Collins Street in the heart of Melbourne. As we were walking, the founder started asking me about my life plans. I told him that I had just quit the law and that I was looking for an opportunity to work in the business community or get an MBA. He looked at me and said, "Why don't you come and work for me?" He mentioned that over the course of the year he had seen me at other networking events for the Australian-African Business Council and had always wanted to talk to me. I was surprised. I wasn't expecting this at all. This had just come out of the blue for me. In that moment, I had to create something for myself. I didn't want to come across as desperate or needy even though I was. I told him that if I came to work for him, I wanted to learn how to be an entrepreneur. I would go to all his meetings and do the follow-up for him. I would be his right-hand man. He agreed. He asked me to come to his office the next day to discuss the role in more detail. I was over the moon. I couldn't believe my next opportunity showed up while doing something that was meaningful to me.

The next day, I walked into the founder's office, and we discussed my role. I created my own position description outlining my specific duties. I became the fourth employee of the educational company. I took a 20 percent salary cut and became the Director of Corporate Affairs. My dream was coming true. The educational company opened doors in all of corporate Australia and around the world. I was twenty-seven years old, and I had become a decision maker in corporate Australia.

Opportunities are everywhere. The question isn't if there are opportunities. The question is if we have the awareness to see the opportunities and the courage to seize them. Leaving the law taught me numerous things:

1. Be intentional. Be crystal clear on who you want to be. I wanted to be a decision maker and help people. You can't fake who you want to be. That is why many people do have impostor syndrome because they are really faking who they want to be. Being intentional requires a high level of authenticity. It is okay not to immediately know who you want to be. The first step is to be willing to be on a journey to find out and allow the process to take time. Who do you want to be?

   **Being intentional requires a high level of authenticity.**

2. Listen to your gut. Your gut is your body's second brain. Exploring being a Property Developer plunged me into a depression. My gut told me no. I listened. What is your gut telling you?

3. Don't let other people define who you are, who you need to be, or what you are capable of. You must define it all for yourself. What others say about you might give you an insight, but it is not the full picture. You must do the work yourself and own who you are for yourself. Corporate Australia told me I was a wild card and so I was a risk to their business. For me being a wild card meant I thought outside the box. I didn't believe that I would be a risk to their business. I knew I would be an asset to any business. I believed that I had experience and wisdom beyond my years and that I could turn mud into gold. What are you capable of?

4. Community is my precious asset. All my opportunities have come because of the community I am in, the networks I have built, and the communities others have willingly shared with me. My community is only as precious as my willingness to be open and vulnerable within it. Who is your community?

5. Shut the back door. The mindset of "being all-in" is different from the mindset of "being half in." New possibilities and opportunities will open when being all-in. Sometimes, being all-in is a gradual process and it's okay to allow ourselves to go through this process. What part of your life are you not "all-in?"

6. Opportunities are found in the things you already love. You must open your eyes and see. You must tell the truth about what you love, not what your parents say you should love, not what society says you should love. I love being a decision maker, I love being the boss, and I love helping people. What do you love?

7. Never give up. Take an action, then take the next action, then the next action, building momentum along the way.

Debrief on what is working and what is not working and explore new possibilities. Then, take the actions inside of the new possibilities, then the next action, until you find what you are looking for. Discover the joy of the journey rather than wait for joy once you reach your desired outcome. The journey is the making of you, the journey is life itself. The outcome is fleeting. Outcomes are results we want to brag about to win people's love and approval. Win your own love. Love your journey of life. That is all you have. What is your next action today?

# CHAPTER 7

# Red Flags and Toxic Workplaces

In the two years that I worked at the company, it became multinational and expanded beyond our wildest dreams. We went on to have hundreds of employees in different countries, including Australia, the United States, Canada, the United Kingdom, and Mauritius. We interviewed presidents, prime ministers, CEOs of Fortune 500 companies, and Nobel Prize winners. As the company grew so did my paychecks and my titles. I started off as the Director of Corporate Affairs, and in time, we added General Counsel.

I felt like a diplomat in the corporate world. During my time, I negotiated several multimillion-dollar deals. My fastest deal took a week. I learned to create deals and close deals without leaving my office or traveling to a new country. I invented partnership models between the company and tertiary institutions. I advised the board from time to time. I resolved legal issues that arose. I worked with managing directors of some of the most prestigious organizations in Australia to navigate accounting, legal, and trademarks around the world. I was involved in projects I had to keep secret to protect former prime ministers and famous people. I was responsible for creating and signing off on the acquisition of the intellectual property of global leaders. The gay Black boy from Mutare, Zimbabwe, had a seat at the table. The only Black man, the only gay Black man, and I wasn't even thirty years old.

## Red Flags

During my two years at this educational company, I learned what it was to be a business leader. I was interacting with people who had power from all around the world, including CEOs, vice-chancellors, and politicians. I was now a decision maker, but something was not quite right. I felt like I was at the pinnacle of the business community, but bit by bit I was becoming unhappy again. There were many signs that something was wrong with the organization, but I ignored all the red flags for money, power, and prestige. Another way of saying it is: "I gaslit my experience of life because I was scared of having no money, power, or prestige."

As I saw the potential of the educational company and the value I could offer, I sought shares in the company as well as remuneration on the value of the partnerships I was creating. To be an equity owner would be a game changer for myself, my family, and future generations. The founder of the company agreed to the plan verbally and in writing. But it was never implemented. I held on to hope that he would keep his promise. I explained his behavior by telling myself he was a busy man. I thought that if I worked harder, I would get his attention. He did not respond to any of my follow-up emails.

**I traded valuing myself for superficial power.**

It's as if the conversation never happened. This was a red flag, but I stayed because I loved the power my role as Director of Corporate Affairs and General Counsel afforded me. It was more power than I had ever had in my life. I traded valuing myself for superficial power.

When the company expanded to America, the founder hired one of his friends to run the American operations. I advised against his hire as the person had no experience nor understood the workings of the American tertiary organization. Not only was he hired, but he would also be working two days a week for a salary of $300,000 while I was working full time and advising him how to grow the American business being paid $80,000. I felt I was not valued for my work and creativity. This was a red flag. I said to myself that I couldn't leave because I had financial obligations. I was responsible for paying half of my sister's school fees, and so having some money was better than having no money. To make me feel better about myself, I told myself that I was making more money than I had ever made as a lawyer, so I should be grateful.

The company had no consistent strategy, and it would change daily. As part of the leadership team of the company, we went on a one-day strategy retreat. It was luxurious and connecting. We ate good food and drank fine wine. As a team, we workshopped an entire strategy together and achieved alignment. We felt we had direction and empowered to fulfill our responsibilities. The next Monday, the founder and CEO of the company went out for coffee, came back, and scrapped the entire strategy with no input nor alignment from the rest of the leadership team. We were shocked. We shouldn't have been, as this had been the behavior of the founder. We were always chasing our tail and were directionless. This was a red flag. But I told myself that I was doing the best I could. What I ignored was the severe negative impact on my mental health. This was a red flag. I explained it away by saying I needed to be tougher like everyone else. I compared myself to others and they seemed to be getting on with the job even if they were unhappy. I felt like a headless chook.

Many of the employees were treated poorly. There was an expectation that when the founder wanted something, it had to happen right then, but you also still needed to finish all the other projects by their deadlines. I remember one of the C-suite executives who had worked for a major airline breaking down with the demands being made on him. He was taking pills to cope. This was a red flag. I told myself that this wouldn't happen to me as I thought I was special. Until it started happening to me. I coped by abusing sex, though at that time, I didn't know I was using sex to numb my pain.

The Foundation was run by white people making a difference in children's lives in Africa. What surprised me was that I was rarely asked for any input regarding strategy implementation. Some of the people on the board of the Foundation had never traveled to an African country. They had no context for the decisions they were making. But I was right here. Many of the attempts that I made to contribute or influence were shut down by the founder. They typically would seek my advice when things weren't working out. I thought it was a stupid way to operate. I am Zimbabwean, with a deep understanding of poverty, drought, HIV epidemics, community structures, and educational systems. Though the Foundation has done some amazing work, it seemed to me that it existed to seem to be doing good rather than do good. This was a red flag. I hate when the Western countries create projects to help Africans but use their efforts more for their own vanity rather than making a difference. The problem with organizations like this is that they do help some people, but it is not their primary focus. Their focus is prestige and fame. The Foundation was no Mother Theresa. So, instead of moan and whine about it, I decided to create my own: the Gomo Foundation.

I started BAM (Black Australian Model) in January 2014. In Australia at that time, there were very few Black "fashion" models, and I decided that I would model and partner with companies and community groups to inspire Black people to be part of the creative space. BAM was divisive. Some people loved a gay Black man modeling and others despised it. One day at work, I got an email that said HR wanted to talk to me. The head of HR looked glum. She told me that I had to stop BAM because they had received a complaint from a manager from a partner institution saying he and the founder did not like it. I was shocked. BAM had nothing to do with the company; it was in my own time. The message I got was, "Don't be too gay, don't be too out there." This was a red flag. I was outraged. Being in a workplace that did not welcome my full self-expression was a red flag. I justified this by telling myself that maybe they were right, that I was the one who was offensive. After all, my job was global and not everyone would like that I was gay.

One of the most stressful times was when I discovered the educational product I was selling to institutions hadn't yet been created. I was negotiating contracts with the promise that we would have a program to deliver by a specific date. As time went on, it seemed that the product wasn't going to be delivered yet my boss kept pressing me to negotiate more deals for something that did not exist. This was a red flag. I told myself that the product wasn't my responsibility; it was a different arm of the business. All I could control was my part, creating and getting the deals done. I felt I was lying to our partners. Nobody else seemed to be worried, so I shouldn't be worried.

## The Wake-Up Call

You would think that all the red flags would wake me up to the toxicity of the company. They didn't. I was so eager to please, so eager to be part of corporate Australia, so desperate to earn money that I didn't even see that I was acting against who I said I was. Perhaps, this is what Uncle Andrew meant when he said he didn't want Australia to corrupt me. This is perhaps why Uncle Andrew didn't want me to stay in Australia, because this worldview was robbing me of health, happiness, and prosperity.

We were working with a creative digital marketing agency. Their work was brilliant, especially the work of Katya. The founder asked me to poach her. Eager to please and produce results, I set off on my mission. I set up a coffee meeting with Katya. I offered her a job at the company. She was delighted. She jumped on board immediately. When I went back to the office, I sent her an email confirming her role and her pay. Her pay would be 20 percent more than what she was getting in her current job.

The next day, waiting in my inbox was an email from the managing director of Katya's company. He was disgusted with the founder and me. He couldn't believe that with everything his company had done for us, we would go behind his back to recruit one of his star employees whom he had spent money, time, and resources in developing to be this star. He had wished that we had approached him first to discuss it. What chilled me to my bones was that he said that he was going to actively go out of his way to communicate what we had done to other businesspeople, so that they would never work with us. Katya had no intention of working for us. Instead, she had used my offer for employment to negotiate a salary increase in her current job. Smart woman. She valued her worth but also valued the company she was working in.

I was terrified. It was only my first two years as a business leader in Australia and I was to be blacklisted. I was over before I had even started. I went straight to the founder's office so that we could respond to the owner of the creative agency. The founder was not interested in responding. I was shaken to my core. I was scared.

I walked back to my seat, slumped down, and allowed myself a few moments to think. I decided to call the managing director of the creative agency on his mobile. As I dialed his number, my heart was pounding. I anticipated him answering the phone and screaming at me. I took full responsibility for trying to poach Katya. I wanted to make sure that he understood that I really understood the harm I did. When he answered the phone and I said my name, he was pissesd off. I took responsibility for going behind his back, for costing his business money, and for breaching his trust. I promised to never do that again. His anger dissipated and he thanked me for my apology.

From that day on, I was awakened to the kind of workplace I was in. My boss did not have my back. He was willing to let my reputation be destroyed. I was working for a person who did not take responsibility for his actions nor considered the impact of his actions as a person of power on others. I was working for a narcissist.

Calling the managing director of the creative agency was the first time I decided what kind of business leader I wanted to be. I wasn't going to use my life anymore to unquestionably please others or to do as I am told without question or turn a blind eye to red flags. I had to confront the truth.

## The Truth

The two years I spent with this company brought me face to face with reality. The truth of the matter is that I wasn't a business leader.

I had titles, I had influence, and I had doors open up for me. But none of this was in my name; it was in the founder's name. I was a messenger, the errand boy. I had been pretending to be a business leader while in fact, I had no idea who I was. I had spent those two years being anything anybody wanted me to be so that I could be part of corporate Australia. I finally understood why I was so unhappy: I had no identity. I had no principles of my own. I thought life was to be lived fulfilling the principles of others, but it never occurred to me to examine whether other people's principles were aligned with my own. Forging my own path in life wasn't just about fulfilling external goals. The missing piece of the puzzle was to determine who I was to be while trying to fulfill those goals.

I am no longer enamored by companies with impressive visions; I am not enamored by the clients a company has worked with; I am not enamored by whether someone knows a president; I am not enamored by whether someone has been on Fox News or ABC News. It doesn't communicate who that person is. All these things society considers success and progress are only half of the story. Who am I enamored by? Warren Buffet. Now that is a business leader, principled to the tee, a man who put in the work, reads, writes, and is principled. He is a man of integrity. He is something I was not. I thought integrity was something outside of me. But integrity and responsibility are something to be found within me.

> I thought integrity was something outside of me. But integrity and responsibility are something to be found within me.

The first value I found for myself by working in this company was integrity. I wanted to be a man of my word. That is the kind of business leader I wanted to be. After two years at the educational company, I negotiated my exit to become who I wanted to be: a business leader. I decided to start my own company so everything would be on my terms. I would no longer hide behind the founder's reputation. It was time to find out who I could be on my own two feet in the world.

# CHAPTER 8

# Becoming Me

January 2015 is when I left the education company to start my own company. Ironically, the educational company became my first client. I negotiated a retainer of $3,000 a month. In addition, for every deal I closed, I would receive a commission of $5,000. Now, in the grand scheme of things, that was peanuts. I was negotiating multimillion-dollar deals. I would continue creating partnerships with tertiary institutions in Australia and around the world. In effect, I was a business developer. I saw this as a transition period, as I set myself up to create my company and the next phase of my life and remove myself from the toxic environment. I set up a family trust. I named it The Mutoko Family Trust. Mutoko is the village where three generations of Gomos grew up: my father, my grandfather, and my great grandfather.

Next, I needed capital in my business. I wrote an email to Uncle Andrew who was living in Scotland and shared my vision for creating my own business, and I requested $50,000 from him. I was upfront with Uncle Andrew that if he were to give me this money, it would be an unsecured loan, and that if I failed, he would lose his money.

Uncle Andrew borrowed the money from a bank in his own name and lent it to me. If I failed and couldn't pay him back, the banks were going to go after his assets. I had no assets. He believed in me unconditionally and unreservedly. I had no evidence or proof if I was going to be successful. Unlike many aspiring businesspeople in Australia who had built-in networks and the comfort of being able to request money from their family and close friends, I only had Uncle Andrew, who was my lifeline.

I had spent two years at the educational company with my objective of learning how to be a businessman, and I felt I'd accomplished that. I'd learned to negotiate deals around the world, network, and how to make money. I'd learned to stand up for myself and I'd learned to manage teams. I learned to be a voice on a board. I had learned so many things about being a businessman that I never would've learned being a lawyer. Being a lawyer taught me the theory of business; being in the educational company taught me the practice of being a businessperson. As I stepped out of the educational company, I was certain I was going to be successful. I had a powerful network, I was not afraid of hard work, and I had a great reputation. What could possibly go wrong?

Within eighteen months, I was close to bankrupt, homeless, and severely depressed.

## The Great Depression

When I started my business, I had absolutely no direction. I didn't know what I wanted to do. There were many things I could do. I could be a lawyer, I could be a business developer, I could be a consultant, I could manage teams, or I can do marketing. I was like a jack of many trades for business. Being able to do many things in business is a good quality, not knowing the primary purpose of why I am creating my business is setting up the business for failure. Because I didn't know what I did, nobody really knew what I did. People didn't know what services to come to me for because I didn't know what I wanted to do. I was plagued with crippling thoughts of failure. I was a Black, gay migrant in Australia, and I had the belief that it would be ten times harder to be successful in white-dominated corporate Australia. I told myself that I needed to get everything right and perfect from day one to be successful. There was no room for error. What if I defined what I did and I failed? I imagined the shame of such failure. I imagined people mocking and laughing at me. I imagined being excluded from net-working events. I imagined people pointing fingers.

**I allowed others to convince me what they thought was the right path. I followed others' ideas because I didn't have my own. The consequences were catastrophic.**

I didn't trust myself. I didn't listen to my gut when I felt very strongly that an idea would not materialize. I would tell myself that maybe they were right. Let's give it a go. There are too many examples of the time, effort, and energy put into ideas that came to naught. A group of friends thought we would begin by creating a coworking space. We thought that a coworking space would be a great way to bring like-minded people together and build our own business community. We spent countless mornings and nights talking about it and planning it, but when push came to shove, none of us wanted to lead it. The sticking point for me is that we didn't have access to capital to pull this off. But I went along for the ride. This idea led to naught. A dear friend and I went to Bengaluru in India for a week to see if we could negotiate deals with Indian tertiary institutions. I didn't know why I was going to India when I knew I could negotiate deals from Australia. Nothing came from the trip. I allowed others to convince me what they thought was the right path. I followed others' ideas because I didn't have my own. The consequences were catastrophic.

\* \* \*

Being directionless was exhausting. Having no direction meant that I entertained all proposals as opportunities. I had no boundaries. I operated "my business" as if I had infinite time and energy.

> **Having no direction meant that I entertained all proposals as opportunities.**

A day in my life looked like this: I would have seven meetings lined up in a day and I'd go from meeting to meeting to meeting. I would share how I would help them negotiate deals to grow their businesses. I would make my notes, then I'd go home, open my laptop to create the deal, and when it came to type it out, I just couldn't. In those moments, I was struck by crippling self-doubt. If I sent a proposal out and they actually said yes that meant that I would be responsible for the delivery of my proposal. What if I failed to deliver? What would happen to me? I was scared! I would say to myself, "Everyone is lying to me. They don't want to work with me. Nobody really wants to work with a Black, gay man from Zimbabwe. They're just being nice and polite." I would then close my laptop, go on my phone, order pork ribs from Uber Eats on my credit card, eat, watch pornography, and go to bed. I'd wake up the next morning and do exactly the same thing. I should have been sending around five to six proposals a week. In six months, I sent out about two proposals. I wasn't making money besides the money I was generating from my first client where I had my $3,000 retainer, and I only closed two other deals. The game in business is to bring in a plethora of opportunities. Nobody's going to do that for you, and I wasn't doing that for myself.

\* \* \*

Another game in business is to bring in more money than you spend. I was spending more money than I was making. I didn't even know I was doing that. I remember one day having a meeting with my book-keeper. She was very concerned. She had asked me if I was going to be able to pay her invoice. I said to her, "Of course I have the money. I've made $6,000 this month." She said to me, "No, you haven't. You have made a loss of $6,000 this month." I argued with her. She explained to me that the brackets around the $6,000 was the accounting terminology for "making a loss." I then said, "Does that mean I've been making a loss for the past six months?" She nodded. All that time, I had been faking that I understood the reports she was emailing me. I didn't know how to read my Profit and Loss statements. I never asked my bookkeeper to teach me as I didn't want to come across as dumb. My pride contributed to my ruin.

**My pride contributed to my ruin.**

\* \* \*

Ruslan Kogan, the founder of Kogan, an Australian retail and services business, proudly said that he had applied for credit cards and used the money to build his empire. I thought that I would solve my money issues by applying for as many credit cards as I could. I already had a $5,000 credit card in my personal name. I applied for a $2,000 credit card with Ignite Virgin. I applied for a $6,000 credit card with

HSBC. Westpac had this amazing offer of a $25,000 credit card for business owners. I leapt at the chance, applied for it, and was successful. "I made it," I thought. I had lines of credit. This gave me lots of breathing room to build my business. When we include Uncle Andrew's money, I had borrowed around $88,000. I ran my entire business and life on borrowed money. There was no financial separation between my personal life and my company. It was just lumped in together.

I thought $88,000 was a lot of money. It seemed to disappear into thin air in no time. I wanted to show the world that I was successful—a successful Black, gay migrant. I wanted to prove to my family that I was successful. I made terrible decisions that depleted all my money. When going out for dinner with friends, I would pay for everyone on my credit card. I wore expensive suits, bought with my credit card, to play the part of being a businessperson. When going out for cocktails, I would pay for all the drinks with my credit card. When it came to paying my sister's university fees, I told my brother I would pay half with money I didn't have just so that my brother would respect me. I thought if people saw me spending money, they would think I have money and business is good. If people thought business was good, they would want to work with me. I was living my life with money I didn't have and making promises I couldn't keep.

There were two questions I would always ask businesspeople and I would universally get the same response. "How are you?" "Good." "How's the business?" "Busy."

I thought being a successful businessperson meant keeping busy. I thought the busier I became, somehow the results would appear. I had never heard a business owner say, "I am not good; I am struggling, I am stressed, I am not coping."

Everything was always fine. Just fine. If I wasn't fine, then there was something wrong with me. I wasn't fine. I thought I was going to die from stress. I was drowning. Nobody could find out I was not okay. This would be a sign of weakness and then nobody would want to do business with me, which would be the ultimate failure. I suffered in silence. As a businessperson, I knew that things would be challenging and difficult, but I had the mindset that things would get better. When I maxed out my first $2,000 credit card, I told myself things would get better. When I maxed out my credit cards for $5,000 and $6,000, I said to myself, "Things would get better." When I maxed out my $25,000 credit card, I still told myself things would get better. I lived in a fantasy that things would get better. Everything was fine, and I kept myself busy.

\* \* \*

By April 2016, it all came to a head. I had maxed out every single credit card. My cash reserves were very low. I had money to last several weeks. I could no longer pretend that I had it together. I was going to be found out for the fraud that I really was. An unsuccessful businessman, masquerading like a successful one.

I was ashamed of myself. I had failed. I had failed my family. I had failed all Black people. I had failed to keep my promise to Jess that we would be great role models for the gay community. I had squandered this precious gift of being Australian. I was facing homelessness, starvation, bankruptcy, and depression. Life was worse than hell. I had never felt so worthless in my life.

\* \* \*

I bought into the fanfare of being a businessperson. The rewards of ultimate freedom, becoming a millionaire, retiring by the time I am forty years old, having enough money to support my family and buy whatever I want, and never having to work ever again. Being a businessperson comes with the false promise of happiness. Yes, all of this is possible, with knowledge, role modeling, mentorship, and experience. I had none of this. Even if I had done everything perfectly, I could still fail. Interest rates may rise, pandemics happen, war breaks out, and you get sued. Choosing to be a businessperson is very brave. When successful, it can be very rewarding, but failure can be catastrophic.

To be a businessperson, I am responsible for everything. The buck stops with me on everything. When things go badly in business, it can lead to financial loss, breakup of relationships, and unimaginable mental health issues. People risk their homes, their relationships, and their children's opportunities with the promise that the pain of running one's own business will lead to unimaginable rewards. However, they say four out of five businesses in the Western world don't make it to their fifth year. We hear these statistics, but we think we are special. We believe we will be that one in five that makes it. After all, our friends and colleagues are saying how smart we are and reassuring us that we will make it.

Taking on being a businessperson was the gift that revealed all my insecurities. I thought I loved myself because I was an out and proud gay Black man. However, taking on being a businessperson revealed my low self-esteem. All the things I had hidden about myself came to light, and I was either going to learn to transform my relationship with myself or have to find a way to cope with the shame.

## Freedom from Debt

Having my life fall apart didn't just affect me. It was affecting all those who relied on me. The first step in cleaning up the mess was first being honest with myself regarding my circumstances. I was not making any money, I did not have money for rent, I could not make repayments toward my credit bills, I could not contribute toward my sister's university fees, I would not have enough money to feed myself, I was not taking the actions required to bring in money into my business.

I opened an Excel document, reviewed my bank statements, and wrote out how I had been spending my money over the past year. My Excel spreadsheet of July 16, 2016, showed that my monthly liability was $9,569.41. When I faced this number, I fell to the ground in shock. My monthly income was around $3,000 per month.

The next step was to deal with all my creditors. I had defaulted on two of the credit cards from my bank. My interest rate payments were around 17 percent, which meant the interest alone for my $25,000 credit card was over $2,000 a month and it kept compounding. I owed the bank more than I had borrowed. Within four months, I owed the bank close to $30,000. My situation felt hopeless. I was terrified of approaching the bank to ask for help because I thought they would take me to court. If I was taken to court, I would have to disclose this to the Legal Services Board and would not be permitted to practice law again. All my investment and hard work to become a lawyer would go down the drain.

**Having my life fall apart didn't just affect me. It was affecting all those who relied on me.**

Instead of paying $30,000 to clear my credit card debt with the bank, they accepted an offer of $13,500. I wouldn't be going through life dragging this humongous debt if I could find a way to pay this off.

I had been here before—I had raised money before. I had to remind myself of what had allowed me to be successful in life. I asked for help. I was vulnerable and open about my life circumstances. I had to do it again. What got me in this situation was pretending I had life handled.

I created a plan. My plan was to raise $2,700 from five people. I only needed five people to lend me $2,700. This felt daunting. I wrote out all the questions I would ask someone if they wanted to borrow money from me. What happened? What is my financial situation? How much do you need? What difference will the money make to your life? When will you pay me back? How am I changing my life so that I am not in this situation again? I spent time answering all these questions before I made any calls. To give myself the best chance of a person saying yes to me, I had to be crystal clear with what I was sharing with them. I formulated my ideal agreement: I would borrow $2,700 with a repayment of $90 a month over thirty months. I would also prepare a proper loan agreement for their records. This payment plan would allow me to live within my means.

I made a list of about thirty people I could call. Within twenty-four hours, I had raised $8,000. I had raised over half of the $13,500 required. I related to myself as a fuckup; yet in the midst of one of the most vulnerable times in my life, my community were willing to rise up and support me. Why did people support me? I told the truth; I had a plan; and I was demonstrating my willingness to change my behavior in the way I approached life.

Not everybody said yes to me when I asked for $2,700. One friend said he didn't have that kind of money, but he offered to donate $500. He didn't want me to pay him back. On the other hand, a very close friend felt that I had violated our relationship by asking for money and putting her in an awkward position to say no to me. I apologized and said to her, "I thought that in our relationship, we could share everything with each other. I'm so sorry that I over-stepped the boundaries." I took full responsibility for placing her in an awkward situation. I also acknowledged that moving forward our relationship did not include the conversation of money. She has never spoken to me again.

I was surprised how easy it was for people to say yes to me. I realized that this could have been how my business had gone if I'd just gone out and made requests and sent out proposals.

In life, many of us are trying to get ahead and cut corners irre-spective of the damage it causes to other people. All the shortcuts we think we are taking chip away at our character—at first slowly and then like an avalanche our entire sense of self collapses. The culture of getting ahead and cutting corners is everywhere: at university when we pay someone to do our assignments, at work when we present our colleagues' ideas as our own, in politics when politicians lie to us regarding what they will do when they get into office. All these shortcuts degrade our sense of self. It's like building a five-story building on sandy land. It will collapse. There are no shortcuts in life. All of us are taking some form of shortcut in life. The question is if we are brave enough to admit we are doing it and face our character head on. As Booker T. Washington said, "Wrong doesn't become right, and evil doesn't become good, just because it's accepted by a majority."[1]

\* \* \*

I was talking to Dad about his relationship with money. He mentioned that when he was a teenager, he had lent money to his brother and his brother didn't repay him. My dad was still enraged as he was telling

---

1    Booker T. Washington, "The Story of My Life and Work," Documenting the American South, University of North Carolina at Chapel Hill, 2004, https://docsouth.unc.edu/neh/washstory/summary.html.

me this story. My dad's brother is dead and yet my dad who is in his seventies is telling the story as if it happened yesterday. Four years after my financial catastrophe, I had never asked my brother if there was anything in the space between him and I. Until my dad's story, I never imagined that there would be anything in the space as my brother always has my back.

Just to make sure, I called my brother who was now living in America to find out if there was anything in the space. He was direct. He said there was. He said that I had promised to repay him for my sister's university fees as well as the money he had given me for my university fees. I was in shock. I asked him how much I owed him. He refused to tell me. He said that what I should be doing instead was coming to him with a check. He sounded really upset, just like my father. I was angry but bit my tongue. I was trying to do the right thing, but I felt thwarted.

I never imagined that my brother would withhold communication with me, as I related to him as a direct person. I felt betrayed. I felt like all this time since university I had been having an inauthentic relationship with my brother. It wasn't real. It was on top of brotherly baggage. The relationship I thought I had with my brother wasn't the relationship I had at all. This realization was one of the most painful moments of my life.

I was horrified that he truly believed that I owed him money for my university fees. During that period in my life, everyone was donating money to me. No one lent me any money. It didn't fit in with my narrative. None of this made any sense to me. I considered the possibility that I was wrong. Seeking my brother's validation and approval could have caused me to make promises I couldn't keep. After all, that is what got me into this financial mess to begin with, particularly around my sister's university fees. I also thought to myself, what is more important here—being in a relationship with my brother or being right? I chose being in a relationship with my brother. Repaying my brother for the money he gave me for my university fees felt like a punishment, and I didn't know what I was being punished for.

After that call with my brother, I went to do some digging. I tracked down any correspondence I had with him involving my university fees as well as my sister's school fees. I checked my Facebook messages back in 2007–2008. None of what I had written spelled anything out in writing like I have today. My communications during that period were unclear. I chose to let go of my point of view regarding payment of university fees. In the scheme of things, this whole conversation wasn't even about money, it was about the kind of human being I wanted to be. I wanted to have authentic relationships—I wanted to take responsibility for where I had failed to keep my promises. That is what I was fighting for with myself in relation to my brother. My investigation indicated that I owed my brother around $36,500. My jaw dropped. That was a lot of money.

On September 20, 2020, I wrote this email to my brother:

*Hi Tendai,*

*Thank you for supporting me during my financial crisis.*

*I don't know how much I owe you. I have gone and reviewed my records, and this is the best I can come up with as an estimation: AU$36,500.00. If it is more, please do let me know.*

*My Uni Fees: AU$7,206.00*

*Ruva's School Fees. My portion is around AU$5,250.00 per year. I paid for Ruva's fees for 2014 and 2015. Therefore, the amount outstanding is $5,250.00 x 4 years = AU$21,000.00*

*Total: AU$28,206.00*

*These amounts do not include ancillary costs like Ruva's flights, accommodation, books. I will estimate that to be another AU$8,000.00 and happy to be guided by you.*

*Proposed Total: AU$36,500.*

## Proposed Repayment

*I have AU$15,000.00 to transfer to you. May you please provide your bank details so that I can make the first payment to you or advise how you wish for me to send you the funds.*

*Outstanding is AU$21,500. I am still formulating a plan for the remainder and will be in communication about this in due course.*

*Thank you,*

*Rugare Gomo*

Having gone through a lot of turmoil in my life, $36,500 would have been useful in "getting ahead." Savings toward a deposit for a house or investing into my business. I repaid my brother every single cent. I made the last payment to my brother on June 21, 2021. On this day, I became debt free. I owed nobody anything. I set myself free. My ongoing amends to my brother is to never ask him for money. I never ever want to get tangled up in that kind of communication again. I only have one brother, and, in this lifetime, I would like it to be the best relationship possible.

I accept that my lack of responsibility regarding my promises negatively impacted my brother. I also accept that despite all my failings in the relationship with my brother, I am not a bad person. I didn't have the tools. I do have the tools now and my living amends is to be clear with my promises, impeccable with my words, and stop being afraid of my brother. I can't control what my brother thinks of me, but I know what I think of me. I am daring; I don't run away from difficult situations; I am authentic; I take responsibility when I fail; I am inspired by who I am. I became free to become me.

I am reborn.

All the bonds of my past are broken.

I am a Phoenix Rising.

DREAMS

# CHAPTER 9

# Being Made to Feel Like I Don't Belong

The world is your oyster. This is not true for me nor for most people. Not all citizenships are equal. I bought into the philosophy that visas are important for a multitude of reasons. They ensure the sovereignty of borders, and they are important to protect the security of nation states. They also protect the citizens who have worked hard, so that noncitizens don't take advantage of them or their resources. I believed in all of this. Not only do these principles sound fair and reasonable, but it's also responsible governance. But the more I traveled the world on my Zimbabwean passport, I learned that these principles were being applied to create opportunity for the "first-world countries" and oppress citizens of "third-world countries."

When most citizens travel to Europe, they hop on a plane with a passport and no questions are asked. However, when I traveled with a Zimbabwean passport, I was made to feel as if I was a threat to national security. I had to prove that I had sufficient funds in my bank account and include a detailed itinerary of where I was staying and for how many days. Any time I wanted to visit Europe, I had to apply for a Schengen visa, which is probably unheard of for most Australian citizens.

I became an Australian citizen on January 26, 2013. In the eyes of the global community, apparently being Australian eliminates me as a security threat. I am deemed fiscally responsible, educated, desirable, and morally good. Endless opportunities are afforded to me, including the holiday visa—an E3 visa that allows me to work in the United States and bring a spouse along. I can renew this visa indefinitely as long as I have employment.

I could go on and on about the privileges that are bestowed upon me for being an Australian citizen: reciprocal healthcare arrangements in Scandinavian countries, my ability to purchase property, borrow money from banks globally, and double tax treaties to prevent me paying double tax. Being Australian affords me power. On my Zimbabwean passport, none of these opportunities are afforded to me. The passport I hold will determine the level of my health, my longevity, my opportunities, and my education. No, we are not equal.

**The passport I hold will determine the level of my health, my longevity, my opportunities, and my education. No, we are not equal.**

For me, I understood the assignment: become an Australian citizen so that I will have access to opportunity. It took me twelve years to accomplish this and to start accessing opportunities that had nothing to do with how smart I am, how hard I worked, how fiscally responsible I am, or how morally good I am. Today, I have more power, more influence, and more opportunity than most of mankind at the detriment of humanity.

There is a rising tide where countries will no longer tolerate the racist and discriminatory practices of developed countries. For example, Brazil has reintroduced visas for Australians traveling to Brazil because the Australian government still requires Brazilian tourists to apply for a visa to visit, while Australians could freely travel to Brazil without a visa. All that President Lula is asking for is equality. The passport I carry today determines the opportunities available to me.

# CHAPTER 10

# Providing Opportunity to Celebrate Self-Worth

## The Black Tax

In 2014, I created the Gomo Foundation, which is a global not-for-profit organization that provides scholarships for girls in Zimbabwe to attend high school. The birth of the Gomo Foundation stems from the fact that corporate Australia remains steadfastly white. The lack of people from diverse backgrounds in positions of leadership, politics, business, schools, and community groups leads to outcomes where many Australian voices are not heard. I was typically the only person in the room with a different perspective to a situation, a different life experience, a different history. Yes, I was raised culturally Anglo-Saxon, I am African, I speak more than one language, and I have grown up being exposed to other cultures other than a Eurocentric worldview. I got to experience the negative consequences of people only raised in one culture. There is even a saying, "to know one culture is to know no culture at all."

The overall view of Africans in Western countries like Australia, the United Kingdom, and the United States is that Africans are very poor and need to be saved. Yes, it is true that many of us on the African continent do not have opportunities like in the West, as we don't have the same standard of education, healthcare, and safety. But what is not talked about are the millions of African diaspora transmitting billions of dollars back home to help their families and communities.

The African nurse who draws your blood for your annual checkup is sending more money than she should to her home country to support her mum and dad. The African engineer who has zero savings because he is paying for his younger brother to attend university in Canada. The African student who is studying full time and working three jobs to pay his own school fees and trying his best to ensure his family has food on the table.

Billions of dollars each year are sent by African migrants to Africa in hopes of alleviating the poverty. And yet, the Africans in Western countries are incapable of growing any wealth because they are still in the cycle of poverty. In Zimbabwe, we call this the Black tax. If your neighbor is African, they are most likely just trying to have a good life in their new country and most of the money they make is likely being sent back home to Africa to keep their family afloat. The Black tax is a phenomenon where we, as African migrants, finally save some money but some life emergency happens back home, and we lose a good portion of it. The Black tax is what keeps us Africans in the cycle of poverty. For many of us, we are not yet in the game of wealth creation. It may look like there is progress because we now have many more Africans who are lawyers, accountants, engineers, doctors, and nurses, but the gap to get ourselves out of poverty is wide.

The Black tax is not specific to us Africans. My Indian, Filipino, Vietnamese, Thai, and Chinese country fellows and many more are doing the same thing. We share the same story. But alas, the nurse, the engineer, and the cleaner are not celebrated for their individual commitments to help eliminate poverty in their communities. Instead, we take more stock in not-for-profits and foundations like World Vision and Save the Children. So, I thought to finally have respect, to help elevate the self-esteem of Black people, my job was to create a not-for-profit organization. I believed this kind of visibility could change the conversation that centers around Black people being takers. I wanted to show that we are givers too. This decision would be rewarding as well as very painful for me.

## The Gomo Foundation

In 2013, my mum was telling me about the work my great uncle, Sekuru Todd, was doing in Ruwangwe, the village my grandmother grew up in. There were many children in the village who did not have access to school, and so Sekuru Todd was spearheading the creation of a secondary school in the village, which was known as Ruwangwe Secondary School. There are many organizations trying to make a difference in Zimbabwe, but this particular project touched me for several reasons. First, the project was in my grandmother's village where I holidayed often when I was a child. When my grandmother was denied an education because she was a woman, the person who benefited was Sekuru Todd. Sekuru Todd was the one who was sent to school because he was a boy. I was touched that he was now using the opportunity given to him to elevate the lives of his community.

In the midst of the Zimbabwean crisis during a time of hyperinflation when there was no food in stores and no fuel, the community wasn't waiting for international donors to help them. The villagers and the children built their own school. The children made the bricks, and the adults created the structure. The village was not waiting for their fortunes to be changed. The villagers were taking charge of their future irrespective of the harsh circumstances in Zimbabwe. I wanted to be part of this. What would be my contribution in elevating the lives of my community?

My family and I decided that we would support two girls to go to school in honor of my grandmother, Mbuya Mutukumira, who herself was denied an education. Still today in Zimbabwe, and in most places around the world, if a family has minimal resources, they will prioritize the boy to go to school. This was the case in the village. In addition, the school fees to send a student to Ruwangwe High School would be $90 a year. For me, living in Australia and earning Australian dollars, $90 a year would be the price of twenty-three chai lattes for a life-changing opportunity for the girls.

I shared the story of Ruwangwe High School with my friend Jess. Jess thought supporting two girls to go to school wasn't enough. She called me out for playing it safe and remaining in my comfort zone. She was right of course. When I thought about the need in the village versus the resources I had, I bumped up against my limiting beliefs. I had a good excuse for not being ambitious. I don't have the money. I am not a millionaire and only wealthy people are able to make that kind of difference, I told myself. I am only a twenty-nine-year-old migrant. An Australian permanent resident, just four years into my professional career. And I have my share of my sister's university fees to pay, the first female in the Gomo family to go to university. I am just starting to build my own life from ground zero. But Jess had planted the seed, and it was gnawing at me.

I looked at the situation from a different angle. I could contribute leadership and knowledge of Ruwangwe and I had a community of wealthy friends and organizations. I knew people who loved making the world a better place. The vision became crystal clear. I could set up a Foundation as a twenty-nine-year old with very little money simply by asking for help. I had done this before. I knew how to do this. After all, I would just have to apply the same principles I had used to raise money for me to go to school.

So, I shared the girls' story with everyone and anyone who would listen to me. And this gave birth to the Gomo Foundation. The purpose of the Foundation was to unleash the potential of girls in Africa through quality education. I recognized that I didn't know much about how to bring this to life. So, the first thing I did was create a Wisdom Council consisting of four people who knew me deeply, loved me, and were well respected in the business community. The second thing I sought was legal advice. I educated myself about what would be required to set up the Foundation, the board, obtaining tax deductibility status, governance, operations, etc. The third thing was creating my team of passionate, intelligent professionals. I shared my vision day in and day out. Each relationship led to the next relationship and then the next relationship. People took on my vision as their own and countless people worked tirelessly to creating opportunities for girls in rural Zimbabwe to have a different life than what they would have without the opportunity.

## Cecelia's Story

In June 2015, I was visiting an organization in Zimbabwe called Cross Reed Investment, a subsidiary of the Red Cross at that time. The CEO shared a story about a high-performing student, named Cecelia, who had just completed high school. Having top marks in the country, Cecelia had earned a place at the University of Zimbabwe to study accounting. However, she couldn't afford $960 for her annual school fees. Instead of going to college, she was living in the village back with her parents, farming the land and living off food handouts.

Cecelia's story is a common one. This is the story of the African continent. So many bright people with no opportunity.

The CEO of Cross Reed Investments asked me if I would help her. I had this pit in my stomach. I personally could not support Cecelia. I already had responsibilities supporting my sister's university fees, which my portion was around $5,000 per year. But I said yes anyway and was immediately filled with fear. I had taken the responsibility for another human being's livelihood and, for me, failure was not an option. Opportunities like this in Zimbabwe are literally life and death. I told myself that I would figure out how to help her once I got back to Australia.

The Gomo Foundation taught me numerous things. One of those things was asking for help. Asking for help has always been difficult, but to accomplish important things in life, I have learned I can't do it alone. Asking for help as a concept sounds simple, but for me, there have always been feelings of failure and shame.

Back in Australia, I shared Cecelia's story with my community and two people agreed to pay her university fees. After four years, Cecelia successfully graduated from university with a degree in accounting. Here is what Cecelia said about having an opportunity to obtain an education:

*"I would like to thank you so much for the great care and contribution toward my education. Now I understand the meaning of life, I understand that I was created for a purpose. I can stand in front of other girls to tell them no matter where they are, where they come from or their background or social life, they can still make it in life. I feel so energized and encouraged. I can never be inferior."*

For me, the Gomo Foundation wasn't just about obtaining an education from books. For me, the Gomo Foundation has always been about empowerment. My experience in life is that knowledge without empowerment is the same as having no education at all. I am so inspired by Cecelia. She has done many hard things. In Zimbabwe, where the unofficial unemployment rate is as high as 90 percent, Cecelia created an internship for herself during her studies. This is empowerment. When Cecelia got her first job after graduating, her boss requested sexual favors if she wanted to keep her job. Cecelia quit the job and found another job in a different city. This is empowerment. This for me has been the success of the Gomo Foundation.

**We focus on acquiring knowledge, yet we don't invest in untapping that knowledge.**

Getting an education can give us access to opportunity. However, in today's world, having an education is not enough. Having a good education as well as having a good relationship with oneself is empowerment. We focus on acquiring knowledge, yet we don't invest in untapping that knowledge. For me, untapping that knowledge means building a healthy relationship with myself and that starts with asking the question, "Who am I?" It requires the courage to give up Mum and

Dad's dreams and hopes for me and instead asking what my dreams and hopes are for *me*. There lies the crossroad to empowerment.

## What Is Philanthropy?

We ran the Gomo Foundation for eight years. Our focus was supporting girls through their six years of secondary school education in Zimbabwe. I had the privilege of observing and experiencing two of the girls start and complete their secondary school and start their university education. The Gomo Foundation had many challenges: raising money, educating people on Zimbabwe, preventing those from importing a Western style governance to our activities in Zimbabwe, my fear of using my voice, my breakdowns in communication between myself and my cofounder, engaging volunteers, running a global organization with no full-time person involved, getting updates about the girls from Zimbabwe where internet is expensive and power cuts are a part of everyday life. Many of these challenges were very painful for me. It felt that the more I tried to grow the organization the more we were distracted from the primary focus, which was about getting girls into secondary school. In 2021, the board and I elected to end the Gomo Foundation and we passed on the projects to another organization called Action on Poverty.

Philanthropy can be good. My desire for an organization that was visible led to my organization spending too much time focusing on what is not important like board meetings, tax deduction status, and governance. The girls in Zimbabwe don't have time for tax deductibility status.

My experience with running the Gomo Foundation changed my thinking. Instead of creating an organization that was separate from me, I pondered how I could fulfill what matters most to me in my everyday life. For me, being part of the change that I want to see in the world requires me to be very specific about the change I want to see in the world. I want to live in an equitable world. Social, economic, and political equity for all people is important to me.

Equity starts with me—in my home, in my workplace, in sports, in my communities, and all around the world. Below is an email I sent to my graphic designer after she sent me an invoice that was too low for the work she had done for me.

*Hi Lisa,*

*Your rate is not aligned with my vision, mission, or values.*

*My vision is to empower and enable people to live a wondrous life. I want you to experience people paying you your worth, not you trying to fit into what you think people can afford.*

*Your rate represents the pay gap between men and women we often talk about. I refuse to talk about it. I choose to take action around it. Your rate would dishonor the women in my life, and I cannot accept it.*

*I want your entire life to work. For your entire life to work, you need resources. Money is one of your resources. It is oxygen to your business and to your life. Currently, with the rate you charge, you are depriving yourself of oxygen.*

*Of course, the conversation of rates will not make any difference until you can see your own worth. You can do this! We all champion you on.*

*Lots of Love,*

*Rugare*

Equity has many different faces. Equity is providing parental leave payments to my team even when my company is not required to do so. Equity is donating to the LGBTQI+ communities that have programs for African migrants. Equity is writing this book and sharing my story because billions of people are like me and don't hear their story in books, or on TV. Equity is saying no to being on a speaking panel of only men. Equity is saying *yes* to giving our First Nations people a voice to have a say over their lives, a power I shouldn't even have. What is equity for you?

To me, philanthropy is living my vision and my values every day in all areas of my life, executing them irrespective of the financial payoff or downside. Executing them when no one is looking. Execute, execute, execute.

# CHAPTER 11

# The Importance of Vulnerability

While I was visiting my family in South Africa, I was mentoring a young woman who had been raped. Her name was Charisa. She was a close family friend and like a sister to me. Tears streamed down her face as she recounted her story to me. Unfortunately, it was not my first time to hear a story like hers. I knew how to help.

My experience of these horror stories on people typically is not only about the incident itself, but also about the narrative we tell ourselves about the incident. I asked Charisa to tell me how she felt about herself. Charisa said she felt worthless, guilty, tainted, unworthy, and shameful. She felt she could not tell anyone because if she did nobody would want to marry her. She was terrified of being ostracized by society for being "impure" and scared of being abandoned by her family. She was in a prison, a living hell. I knew these kinds of feelings all too well.

Charisa wanted to be free and be happy again. Together, we speculated what freedom could look like. The obvious first step to freedom would be to stop internalizing that she was sexually abused as a dirty secret. We explored together what actions she felt empowered to take to lift the shame. She decided to tell her aunt in Canada.

After Charisa went home, I went to my room, closed the door, called my business partner back in Australia, and cried my eyes out. I was devastated that this beautiful, twenty-one-year-old young woman had been violated. I was angry at men for what they think is their entitlement. Those men who still think it is their right to possess women. Those men who think they have a say in how a woman should use or not use her body. Those hypocritical men who talk about family values but behind closed doors are going to strip clubs, having affairs, and bringing diseases back to their family. I cried for all the women of the world that night.

The next morning, I heard a lot of commotion downstairs. It sounded like my mom's voice and another woman. Then, I heard someone stomping up the stairs. I heard a knock on my bedroom door. I told them to enter. It was Charisa. She plonked herself onto my bed and declared boldly with a beaming smile: "I am free." Charisa said she had told her aunt everything that had happened to her. Charisa's act of courage to share something that was so vulnerable had set her free. She had physically transformed. She was making eye contact with me and speaking to me as her peer. Her beautiful, chocolaty face glowed. She had stopped trying to make her body small. Her presence consumed the space in my bedroom. We celebrated.

I returned to Australia the following week. I made Charisa a promise that whenever she needed someone to talk to, she could always call me, and I would get back to her as soon as I could. I reminded Charisa that freedom is a continuous act and that she would still need to continue taking actions for freedom in this area of her life. It is so easy to fall back into the same old stories about ourselves if we are not vigilant to nurture our new freedom.

A few weeks later, I received a WhatsApp message from her. She said she was now ready to tell her dad and her stepmom. I asked her if she needed anything. She said no. In addition, I asked for Charisa's permission to share with my mum and dad what was happening as I suspected that once Charisa's parents knew what was happening, they would seek counsel from my parents. And they did.

Sexual violence against women in South Africa is one of the highest recorded in the world. Several months later, Charisa informed me that she was participating in a march at the University of Pretoria protesting against sexual abuse against women on campus. It is mind-boggling to see Charisa's transformation from being a downcast young woman and making herself small to using her voice and freely sharing her story. Charisa was free from the story of what happened to her. Today, she has graduated from law school and is a lawyer.

Charisa's story is one of many I've witnessed over the years. We all have a narrative that prevents us from moving forward and expanding who we have the potential to be.

## Steps to Freedom: A New Way of Living

Like Charisa, there are certain steps to take to achieve freedom from your past. There are so many ways to be free. There isn't just one way, but here is one I use in my everyday life to set myself free.

Firstly, write out the entire story, your thoughts, your feelings, and the decisions you made about yourself, others, and the world. Writing out the story is important because it gives physicality to what has been twirling in your head for days or weeks, if not for years.

Secondly, start separating the facts from the story. In Charisa's example, it is a fact that she was raped. It is a story that she is tainted, unworthy, and impure. Separating the facts from the story gives us the opportunity to act on what is real versus what is not.

Thirdly, speculate what freedom is for you now. It is an inquiry. An inquiry is an exploration. It is a journey one goes through without knowing what the answer will be. To be free requires us to have an open mind. Speculating is a creative process, so write everything that comes to mind without judging it. Allow yourself to explore the infinite possibilities of what freedom could be.

Fourthly, take actions to be free. For Charisa, freedom started by sharing with me she was raped. It grew when she told her aunt in Canada. Then, several weeks later, Charisa had the freedom to share with her dad and stepmom. Charisa protesting the violence of women was an act of freedom. Knowing the actions to be free is not freedom. Freedom is to be found in taking the actions consistent with freedom.

Lastly, celebrate, celebrate, celebrate. Celebrate every time you take an action to be free. To be free requires work and requires you to be disciplined, but to be free is brave. It is easier to complain and remain in the story and it is easier to be the victim of the stories we tell ourselves. It is harder to be brave like Charisa, who, without knowing what the predetermined external outcomes would be, took actions to be free.

My learning about freedom is that the outcomes of freedom are the outcomes of freedom. Another way to say it is that I may have my preconceived idea of what should happen or what I would like to have happen if I take certain actions, but my experience is that to be truly free, I let go of all my preconceived ideas and take actions consistent with freedom and more will be revealed. Most of the time, even more wondrous outcomes than I could ever imagine reveal themselves. In Charisa's case, she was able to receive love and use her voice to support other people like her.

There are no half measures to freedom. There isn't a cheat sheet to freedom. We either do the work to be free or we are not free. This can be quite confronting, and for many people, it is easier to remain with what is familiar. I empathize. But I ask you today, will you dare to set yourself free?

## Being Free Is a New Identity

I never dreamed of being a high-performance life and business coach. Since I'd never met a coach before, it had never been something that was modeled for me. I thought coaches were for people failing in life. In 2014, I learned about coaching in a personal development program, and I saw the direct impact coaching had on people's lives. I knew right away that I wanted to be a part of this transformation, and for about three years straight, I practiced my craft day in and day out.

In December 2018, my best friend Luke Galea and I started two companies: Simbisa Law and our coaching business Kukura International. We grew these companies together for two years until Luke decided he wanted to change his path in life. I took over both companies. Working with Luke was very empowering. We had a clear vision, we knew the people we served, and we empowered each other to be the greatest versions of ourselves. The coaching business always outperformed the law firm, and I didn't know why. I read the book *Profit First* by Mike Michalowicz. I had to confront that my law firm was unprofitable and eating all the money from the coaching business. I didn't want to have another financial catastrophe. I was at a cross-roads as I was scared to give up my identity as a lawyer. I believed that my clients chose me as a coach because I was also a lawyer. There are so many coaches out there in the world and I thought that being a lawyer is what was distinguishing me from the masses. Who would I be without the identity of lawyer? I would just be a high-performance coach. How would my mum and dad explain to their friends what I did? "My son is a high-performance coach" simply did not have the same ring as "My son is a lawyer."

Reviewing another shareholder's agreement wasn't helping people lead better lives. Clients wanting me to reduce my already low legal fees to help them set up a company wasn't making the world a better place. There are already too many lawyers, better lawyers than I would ever be. The truth of the matter is that my law firm was failing because I did not believe in it. It wasn't making the kind of difference I saw possible. I didn't want to fix people's legal problems as a lawyer. I wanted to be part of the movement that focused on awakening people to their unique greatness. I was very good at having conversations to empower people to be the author of their own life. I was being sought after to share my failings, mistakes, and successes in life and business, and people's lives were being changed for the better. This for me was meaningful work and it made me feel good. I gave up the practice of law and surrendered fully to who I truly wanted to be: a high-performance life and business coach.

What lights me up are the courageous stories of my clients who dared to forge their own path in life. A client said to me: "I sold my chicken shop and I now have time to spend with my family." An owner of a law firm said to me: "I thought I would be free when I was in my sixties. I didn't know I could be free in my forties." A father whose daughter had died said to me: "I have found joy doing what I love even though my daughter is dead." My engineering client who started with debt said to me: "My company made four million dollars this year." A wife said to me: "You saved my marriage."

What I have learned by being a practitioner of freedom is that every time I reach some sort of crossroad, there is a little voice in my head that pops up to destroy what is possible for me. It rears its ugly head by sounding logical and reasonable by asking questions like, "Will I be able to make enough money to support myself? Do you really want to start from the bottom? Will I really be happier on this new path?" The voice attempts to talk me out of pursuing what I saw is possible for myself. It tells me that the path I am already on is safer.

I have never been able to eradicate this little voice. I have come to recognize it as part of my humanity. However, I now know this little voice in my head isn't truth. It is the voice of fear. Fear keeps me imprisoned. Today, when fear strikes, I ask myself what freedom is for me today and take an action toward freedom. The more actions I take, this little voice becomes smaller and smaller and smaller. Being free is possible for you. Be brave and take an action of freedom today.

# CHAPTER 12

# Finding Love

In the past, whenever anyone showed me any attention, affection, or intimacy, I clung onto it like my life depended on it. I have been completely and utterly satisfied with any crumbs of intimacy and never really examined whether the relationships I was getting into were healthy and life giving.

I no longer wanted the crumbs of intimacy. I wanted it all. I could have it all. I deserved to have deep, profound, loving, genuine, respectful, healthy intimacy and connection in my life and I would have it. I drew the line in the sand. I declared to myself that I wanted to have a relationship that provides for my emotional, spiritual, intellectual, sexual, and physical needs.

I used to be profoundly ashamed of my failure to remain in the Disney fairy-tale of the happily-ever-after standard and ideal of a romantic relationship. I used to date people who made me feel good about myself. I used to date people I could fix. I used to date people who I thought were popular and liked by others even if I didn't like them. All this dysfunction in my relationships was because I did not like myself. I was using relationships to fix my low self-esteem and self-hatred. The antidote isn't taking a partner as a hostage. Instead, the antidote is to heal trauma.

With lots of therapy and working a Twelve-Step Program, I learned to love myself. Over time, my self-loathing became smaller and smaller, and my self-esteem and self-respect grew. I learned to love myself and my relationships became healthier and enriching.

The more I loved myself, I was able to speak my truth, set and maintain boundaries, resolve conflicts rather than avoid conflicts, and communicate my emotional, intellectual, and sexual needs. The more I learned to love myself, my choices and those who chose me became healthier. From time to time, I can have moments when I hate myself. The difference today is that I know these thoughts are not true and the feelings will pass.

Today, I am grateful for every romantic relationship I've ever had. Most of them have been totally awful and horrible. Yet, all of them—yes, all of them—brought me closer and closer to myself. They led me to discover who I am and who I want to be. They have taught me to articulate my needs and my wants. They have shown me what brings me horror and what allows my heart to experience exquisite joy. And I did find exquisite joy.

## Falling in Love

His name is Higor. I fell in love with him on April 25, 2023, and proposed to him on June 25, 2023. I wrote a letter to the love of my life and left it on our lounge table with his name on it. I sat on the opposite chair and watched him read it.

Dear Higor,

The greatest gift I can give you are my words and my time.

So here is my most precious gift to you.

You have given me the honor to be your boyfriend, an honor I do not take lightly.

I will do my best to love you.

I will do my best to treat you as the king you are.

I will do my best to support you.

I will do my best to listen to you.

I will do my best to always resolve any conflict from love.

I will do my best to keep you safe.

I will do my best to inspire your spirit and heart.

I will do my best to bring God into our relationship each day, each hour, each second, each moment.

I am a very flawed human being. I have made many mistakes in my life. My greatest fear I have faced to date is to love you.

In my view of myself, there is no evidence that I can be a good boyfriend to you. I feel like I have always failed, and I turned to my God and I faced my fear.

I faced my fear to love you and to receive your love.

I faced my fear to share my life with you.

I faced my fear to reveal my true self to you and have it accepted or rejected.

So, because of you, my life and my experience of the universe grew a trillion times.

Thank you for loving me first.

Thank you for being open first.

Thank you for showing me who you are first.

Thank you for accepting and loving me first.

Thank you for risking being heartbroken by showing me your beauty first.

As we embark on the journey of sharing our life together, everything of our lives, the good, the bad, the ugly, the love, the pain, the despair, in sickness and in health, this is my desire for us:

We started the relationship in **freedom**, and I wish for us always to feel and experience freedom.

We started the relationship being **bold and courageous**. I desire that we co-create our lives always from being bold and courageous.

We started the relationship growing our **connection** and having intimacy. I think our relationship can be magical if we continue to be intimate with each other. I don't mean sex; I mean that feeling of closeness, safety, freedom, and love.

We started the relationship with having **supernatural sex**. Yes! Let us continue doing that.

We started the relationship by being **vulnerable**, sharing our needs and respecting them. You never shamed me for being special. Let us continue creating a safe space for each other.

You and I are not like everyone else: We are migrants. We are people of color. We have come from religious families. We both know poverty. We both understood the prejudices in this world. Yet, both of us do not live our lives as victims to our circumstances. We both have created our own path and many doors have opened for us. Individually, we are already successful, and our lives will be good. I want our relationship to be magical for you. And I also want to uplift people like us to know that they too can live in freedom.

We still live in a world where many gay people lose their parents, lose their lives because they are gay. Many gay people still live in fear because of who God created them to be; I used to be one of them. I lived in utter fear! Unfortunately, as a result, I still suffer the consequences of that which I work on in my recovery program so that I can be the best person for you and the world.

I want us to be always free. Our happiness, our lives depend on it. Let's never hide our true selves from ourselves or each other. Let's always be free no matter what.

I don't know what the future holds, but I have many dreams for us: Dreams of travel. Dreams of adventure. Dreams of an abundant life. Dreams of experiencing things most people never experience. Dreams of praying together. Dreams of growing old joyously together. Dreams of helping many people around the world.

I dream. And all that matters is the gift of a new day and being present with you each day, and seeing where our God will take us. That is enough. I am happy to be poor with you materially, and I am happy to be sick with you. What matters is we are doing it together, and that is God's will for us.

My Man, my Beautiful Man. I never expected to fall in love. I didn't see myself as capable of a romantic relationship, but your love paved the way. It's like all my life I have been getting ready to meet you. I have been waiting for you all my life. The journey to love you has been one of my most difficult, but it is a treasure, a precious gift.

You are my most precious gift. To God and to you, I am grateful.

You have given me the honor to be your boyfriend. I now humbly bow before you, Higor Rezende, and ask you if you will give me the honor to be your husband. Will you marry me and continue creating memories together?

Rugare Gomo

Higor gasped toward the end of the letter. He stood up and said, "I accept." He fell on bended knee and proposed to me too. I accepted. I pulled him up. We hugged. Higor cried in my embrace as we started a new phase of life together.

In our lifetime, neither of us thought we would find love. The boy from Mutare, Zimbabwe, and the boy from Goiânia, Brazil, found love in one of the most beautiful places on Earth: Sydney, Australia.

# CHAPTER 13

# Forging My Own Path: A Blueprint for Living

In all my adventures, I've never known how to articulate what happiness means to me.

I thought if I became an Australian lawyer, I would be happy. I wasn't!

I thought that if I became an Australian citizen, all my problems in life would disappear and I would be very happy. I wasn't!

I thought that now that I have started my own law firm, I will surely be happy. I wasn't!

I thought that if I came out and shared with the entire world that I am a gay man, I would surely be happy. I wasn't!

I thought that if I had lots of sex and many people wanted to have lots of sex with me, I would absolutely be happy. I wasn't!

I thought that if I was embracing all the opportunities provided to me that are not provided to most Black, gay migrants, I would be happy. I wasn't!

I thought that if I was volunteering my time to help people "less fortunate" than me, I would then be happy. I wasn't!

I have done it all. I've changed nationalities and countries; learned another language; absorbed multiple cultures; traveled the world; made money; helped thousands of people; volunteered my time, energy, and mind; had lots of sex; and entered into so many different kinds of relationships. I've been recognized, won awards, and became highly educated. I have started organizations and companies, I have sat on boards, I have been self-sacrificing and gone into debt for my family and loved ones, I have tithed, I have met prime ministers and ambassadors, and I have dined with billionaire families. I've been the good boy and the bad boy.

The more I accomplished, the more I achieved, the worse my life became. As we say in French, "j'ai perdu l'envie de vivre"—*I lost the desire to live.* I had never felt this depth of hopelessness before. I thought I was not happy because I wasn't ambitious enough. So, I had to do more. Only once I accomplished the next big thing, I would be happy. Every time I pursued the next big thing, my life became worse. I was more stressed, more anxious, more fearful, more depressed. And I pretended that I had it handled. My life was completely unmanageable. Is this what I left Zimbabwe for? It felt like my life was worse living in Australia rather than had I stayed in Zimbabwe. This can't be the Australian dream.

To make matters worse, everyone seemed to be doing exactly what I was doing, so I thought then that there was something wrong with me. That became my prison. This made no sense to me. I have accomplished more than most people twice over and I was profoundly unhappy. I couldn't seem to figure it out.

On my journey to forging my own path in life, I had always been looking for a formula for living. My formula was rooted in dreaming big, doing more and being more. More, more, more. My approach to life had become bankrupt. I had used my entire life to survive, strive, and overcome adversity. It was all I knew. This approach to life was robbing me of my health, happiness, and prosperity. I had to discover a new, empowered way of living.

I was born into a world that has rules, and many of those rules were not made for me: don't be gay; boys don't cry; read your Bible every day. The list goes on and on. I am very skeptical about dogmatic approaches to anything. Every human being is unique. I am unique. You are unique. I don't believe the answer to living life is to be found in rules or in dogma. I believe the answer to living an empowered life has always been inside of me. I was born free. It was the world that told me that I couldn't be. The answers to freedom are all around me. The key to freedom was in all things: the good, the bad, the ugly. I found the key to living an empowered life:

> **Life could be simple and easy. In this life, I could be happy.**

1. *Reality:* To have power in life, you must train yourself to be able to distinguish what is real (the facts) versus your interpretation of reality (the story).

2. *Authenticity:* Opportunity correlates to your willingness to be vulnerable, open, and transparent.

3. *Creativity:* There isn't one way to respond to life. There are infinite possibilities to respond to any situation in life. You are free because you get to choose how to respond.

4. *Your Word:* Fulfilling on what you say, and who you say you are, is who you are for that moment.

5. *Actions:* Results are a function of action, so act now.

6. *Responsibility:* You are responsible for what you say, who you are, and what you do. You are not responsible for outcomes and results. Surrender outcomes and results to the universe.

7. *Love:* Discover love in everything. In love, you are free.

What did this framework of life make available for my experience of life? Freedom, peace of mind, self-expression, and love. Life could be simple and easy. In this life, I could be happy.

# This Is My Story

I am a storyteller
My mum is a storyteller
My grandmothers are storytellers
My ancestors are storytellers
In my culture, wisdom is passed from generation to generation
through stories
Story time is after diner time, just before going to bed
Going to bed is a time to reflect on the stories

Story time is everything
A time for hope
A time for inspiration
A time to instill fear
A time to meditate
A time to connect
A time to learn
A time to ask questions

Story time is everything
Story time is like entering the metaverse
There are no human rules in story land
Yet, the stories always have some poignant life lesson


I am not the first life coach
All my ancestors are life coaches
They shared stories and transmitted their experience,
      strength and hope to all who keenly listen
There is no depression because we have stories,
      we are mentally healthy
There is no disconnection because we have stories,
      we have community
There is no confusion because we have stories, we have wisdom
Our stories are life


We sit around the fire and my grandmother tells us all sorts of
stories
Mum is finding opportunities to share stories
Mum is telling stories when we roast the nuts at the fireplace
Mum is telling a story while we are sewing together
Mum is telling stories when washing the dishes
Mum is telling a story when we sit on the couch
      drinking a cup of tea
Mum is telling a story in the car on our family holiday adventure
There is always a story around the corner
I am completely enamored by the stories
I feel whole
I feel complete
I feel alive

I feel more capable to approach life as I walk in the shoes of those
      who carry me and come before me
My uncles, my aunts, my cousins, my village, my country
      are all telling stories
I listen, I grow, I transform
I take what works for me and discard what doesn't work for me
Sekuru Todd, my great uncle, calls me the "why" boy
I am constantly asking why
I am never shamed for asking why
Why is the beginning of a story
Why is the beginning of multiple stories
Why is the beginning of entering the metaverse
No story ever ends because of Why
Because of Why, I am
Because of Why, I be
Because of Why, I feel
Because of Why, I am connected to all things
I now see, there is no beginning and there is no
end to the stories because of Why

Storytelling is not just a good idea, it is my responsibility
To stop stories is to break the link to my ancestors
To stop stories is like burning books
To stop stories is to erase one's own existence
To tell stories is oxygen
To tell stories is my only hope to live a full life
To tell stories is to be limitless
To tell stories is to pass on what is freely given to me
The health, happiness, and prosperity of the human race
      requires I tell THE story

The Europeans have ensured their stories live on forever and
      have ensured that the rest of the world pays for it. How?
Through Classical music, we listen to Beethoven, Mozart.
      Concert halls, opera houses are built all around the world
Through Literature, we read Shakespeare, Voltaire, Charles Dickens
      to be taught in schools all around the world
Through TV, we watch *Vikings*, *Emily in Paris*, *Game of Thrones*
      on TV sets all around the world
Through Art, the preservation of the *Mona Lisa*, Picasso,
      Artemisia Gentileschi. Art in art galleries around the world
The entire education system is built on passing down the stories
      of Europeans, creating a European hegemony
The European hegemony buries the Arab stories, the Asian stories,
      the African stories, the First Nation stories
The European hegemony drowns the voice of my mother
The European hegemony erases the stories of my grandmother
The European hegemony silences the voices of my ancestors
My sickness begins
I don't know who I am, the story is erased from my history
I don't know who to be, the story is buried
I don't know how to think, the story has disappeared
      from the consciousness of the metaverse
I may never find the story ever again
There is a gaping wound in my soul
I live my life always feeling that there is something missing
      inside of me
The story is weeping to be told

Now what?

I refuse to be subjugated

I break free

I shall follow in the footsteps of my mother,
        my grandmother, my village, my country

I start sharing my story

I will share my story to everyone

Everyone will hear my story

Perhaps, what has been silenced will be awakened

Maybe you start sharing your story

Maybe those after me use their voice and share their story

Maybe we restore the health, happiness, and prosperity of humanity
        as the hegemony is broken

I finally hear Arab stories

I finally hear African stories

I finally hear Asian stories

I finally hear First Nation stories

I finally hear 7 billion stories

The metaverse is whole again


My name is Rugare Gomo

And this is my story

---

# with Rugare Gomo

Rugare Gomo would be delighted to connect with his readers professionally and socially!

WEBSITE: www.rugaregomo.com

LINKEDIN: linkedin.com/in/rugaregomo

YOUTUBE: www.youtube.com/@rugare_gomo

FACEBOOK: facebook.com/rugaregomo

INSTAGRAM: instagram.com/rugaregomo

For professional and media inquiries, speaking engagements, coaching services, and questions about Dreams: Forging my Own Path, you can reach Rugare Gomo directly at connect@rugaregomo.com.

www.ingramcontent.com/pod-product-compliance
Lightning Source LLC
Chambersburg PA
CBHW021231090426
42740CB00006B/482